Jobseeker's Guide
Sixth Edition *by*
Kathryn Troutman

Training Handout for Ten Steps to a Federal Job® Workshops

The
Resume Place

Catonsville, MD 21228
www.resume-place.com

The Resume Place, Inc.
Federal Career Publishers

P.O. Box 21275, Catonsville, MD 21228
Phone: 888-480-8265
www.resume-place.com
Email: resume@resume-place.com

Printed in the United States of America

Jobseeker's Guide, 6th Ed.
ISBN: 978-0-9846671-4-7
Updated April 2014

We have been careful to provide accurate federal job search information in this book, but it is possible that errors and omissions may have been introduced.

Attention Transition Counselors, Veterans' Representatives, Workforce Counselors, Career Counselors: The *Jobseeker's Guide* is a training program "handout" to support the Ten Steps to a Federal Job® workshops and PowerPoint program, which is taught at military bases, universities, one-stops, and DoD agencies worldwide. To be licensed to teach the Ten Steps to a Federal Job® curriculum as a Certified Federal Job Search Trainer™ or Certified Federal Career Coach, go to www.resume-place.com for information on our train the trainer program. Since the program was developed in 2002, more than 1,000 have been licensed to teach Ten Steps to a Federal Job® with this guide as the handout.

AUTHOR'S NOTES: Sample resumes are real but fictionalized. All federal applicants have given permission for their resumes to be used as samples for this publication.
Privacy policy is strictly enforced.

PUBLICATION TEAM
Cover, Interior Page Design, and Developmental Editing: Paulina Chen
Federal Resume Samples: Kathryn Troutman, Emily Troutman, Ellen Lazarus, Carla Waskiewicz, Lee Patterson, Kristin Mianecki, Dawn McClure, Richard Cruikshank, Toran Gaal
Contributors: Margaret F. Dikel, Ellen Lazarus, Dennis Eley, Jr., Lawrence Kimble, Troy Johnson, John Gagnon
Wounded Warrior Technical Consultant: Dennis Eley, Jr., Wounded Warrior Coordinator, OCHR-San Diego Ops Center
Human Resources Technical Consultant: Ellen Lazarus, J.D., Retired Senior Federal Manager
Copyeditor: Pamela Sikora
Indexer: Christine Frank

"Over the past decade, nearly 3 million service members have transitioned back to civilian life, and more are joining them every day.

"When these men and women come home, they bring unparalleled skills and experience. ... They've saved lives in some of the toughest conditions imaginable. They've managed convoys and moved tons of equipment over dangerous terrain. They've tracked millions of dollars of military assets. They've handled pieces of equipment that are worth tens of millions of dollars. They do incredible work. Nobody is more skilled, more precise, more diligent, more disciplined.

"... These are the Americans we want to keep serving here at home as we rebuild this country. So we're going to do everything we can to make sure that when our troops come home, they come home to new jobs and new opportunities and new ways to serve their country."

– President Obama, February 3, 2012
Remarks at Fire Station 5, Arlington, Virginia

Dear Federal Jobseekers, Employment Readiness Specialists, Transition Specialists, Career Counselors, and Ten Step Trainers,

Since our last edition of the *Jobseeker's Guide*, the federal government has continued to be the "Employer of Preference" for transitioning military, veterans, military spouses, and Wounded Warriors. A White House Press Release* states: "the first two quarters of FY2013, 35.1 percent of all new federal hires were veterans."

At the same time, the number of jobless veterans continues to outpace that of civilians. Federal jobs remain one of the most important resources available to separating and retiring personnel, but the system for applying is incredibly complex.

This sixth edition of the *Jobseeker's Guide* focuses on making the federal application process as understandable as possible. This 6th Edition now includes:

- Before & After federal resumes for a new transitioning Navy Seabee who left the Navy service early due to the Enlisted Retention Board (ERB) and landed a fantastic career ladder position as Occupational Safety & Health Specialist

- Before & After federal resumes for a Wounded Warrior who wrote a short description of his Wounded Warrior Transition activities and summarized his previous military history and education

- The 11 Point CheckSheet review for the "before" resume in each case study

- Five ways to write up the Wounded Warrior transition time period in a resume

- New information on Federal Hiring Programs: PPP-S for spouses in the US; Title 32 Dual Status Technician Positions; Pathways Internships; Wounded Warrior Resume Writing Tips; Schedule A Hiring Programs

- The latest USAJOBS application information

This book is written especially for transitioning military, veterans, military spouses, Wounded Warriors, as well as Army, Marine Corps, Navy, Air Force, Coast Guard, National Guard, and Air National Guard Employment Readiness Specialists, and Transition Specialists who are teaching the Ten Steps to a Federal Job® workshop at military bases worldwide.

I hope to see you soon in one of our classes.

Good luck with your federal job search,
Kathryn Troutman, Author and Publisher

* http://www.whitehouse.gov/the-press-office/2013/08/10/
fact-sheet-obama-administration-s-work-honor-our-military-families-and-v

How Many Hats Do You Wear at Work?

Everyone wears different "hats" at work. The hats you wear at work are KEYWORDS for your federal resume. Make a list of 5 to 7 hats you wear every day in your job. This exercise will help you write your federal resume with keywords (nouns and verbs) in the Outline Format. See more information in Step 5 on keywords and in Step 6 on federal resume writing in the Outline Format.

Examples of hats:

- *Supply Analyst*
- *Logistics Manager*
- *Transportation Specialist*
- *Supervisor*
- *Instructor*
- *Team Leader*
- *Database Administrator*
- *Research / Analyst*
- *Contract Officer*
- *Purchasing Specialist*
- *Office Administrator*
- *Advisor*
- *Computer Operations*

Your list of 5-7 hats:

_____

_____

_____

_____

_____

_____

_____

The Ten Steps to a Federal Job® are a proven successful campaign strategy to LAND a federal job. It takes attention to detail, learning about federal employment, and analytical skills to match your resume to a specific job title or announcement. With perseverance, your chances of getting Eligible, Best Qualified, Referred, Interviewed, and HIRED are much higher with this method.

1. **Review the federal job process.** Start your federal job search with critical federal job information. Find out which agencies, job titles, and grade levels are best suited for you.

2. **Network.** Even with government, who you know is important. This information will remind you that your family, friends, and acquaintances may be a lead to a job in government. Learn strategies to introduce yourself and your job goals.

3. **Research vacancy announcements on USAJOBS.** Learn the fastest way to search for federal jobs on USAJOBS. Search for geographic location and salary first, then drill down to the jobs that sound right for you. You can't write a good federal resume without a target vacancy announcement— even if the announcement is a sample to get you started.

4. **Analyze your core competencies.** In addition to technical keywords and qualifications, your basic core competencies can help you stand out. Are you flexible, customer-focused, and creative? Do you demonstrate excellent team membership abilities, and work well under deadlines? Technical, specialized skills + great interpersonal skills = Best Qualified!

5. **Analyze vacancy announcements for keywords.** Learn how to find keywords in each announcement for your federal resume. Look for the keywords in Duties, Qualifications, Specialized Experience, and KSA lists. Add the keywords into your resume to make it readable, focused, and impressive.

6. **Write your Outline Format and paper federal resumes.** Feature your top skills and accomplishments for each position with keywords. Master the two formats: the Outline Format for online builders, and the paper format for interviews, email attachments, and browser uploads.

7. **KSAs in your federal resume and assessment questionnaires.** The "rated and ranked" KSAs have been eliminated, but various "how to apply" instructions may still list KSAs that should be covered in the resume. You will also find Assessment Questionnaires with Yes/No and multiple-choice questions.

8. **Apply for jobs with automated recruitment systems.** Carefully read the "how to apply" instructions, which could be different for each announcement. Get ready to copy and paste your resume into builders, answer questions, write short essays, and fax or upload your documents.

9. **Track and follow up your applications.** Don't just send in your application and forget about it; you have to manage your federal job search campaign. Learn how to call the personnel office to find out critical information for improving your future applications. Find out how to get your application score.

10. **Interview for a federal job.** Get tips to improve your chances with different types of interviews. Tell your best stories about your accomplishments and leadership skills. Be personable, passionate about the job, and sharp with our list of techniques.

Take a few minutes to write your information and accomplishments.

Please answer these questions:

What is your current or last job title?

Accomplishment Freewriting:

Describe an accomplishment from your current position or recent volunteer work. Accomplishments are critical for your federal resume, assessment questionnaire essays / examples, and behavior-based interviews.

Write at least three sentences here about your accomplishment:

_____

_____

_____

_____

_____

_____

Here are two federal resume sections demonstrating how to feature both your Duties and your Accomplishments in each job in your resume. Adding accomplishments into two or three of the positions in your Work Experience section will make your resume stand out.

WORK EXPERIENCE – VETERAN

Operations Officer, 1st Cavalry, Ft. Hood (Forward Deployed to Iraq), TX, 2008

PLANNING AND ORGANIZING WORK. Over a period of fifteen months, during the Surge, directed and scheduled the aerial logistical movement of 55,600+ passengers and 7.915M+ pounds of equipment in hostile overseas environment.

INTERPRETING PROGRAM REQUIREMENTS. Researched, coordinated, and developed logistical support plans, instructions, and guidelines for 110+ aircraft in support of 10+ Brigade Combat Teams conducting reconnaissance and attack missions, logistical resupply, and patient evacuation missions across Iraq.

SIGNIFICANT ACCOMPLISHMENTS:

- Recognized by senior executives for successfully raising the performance and morale of a 23-person cross-functional team across 8 distinct occupations. Accomplished this by taking a personal and professional (job) interest in each soldier and by establishing a daily shift change brief for synchronization and dissemination of information, which helped to reduce general anxiety, questions, and the general fog of war.
- Recognized by supervisor for exceeding expectations and recognized as being the best Medical Service Corps Officer he had met in his 22 years of service. Received Bronze Star medal for exceptionally meritorious service.

WORK EXPERIENCE – MILITARY SPOUSE

INDIVIDUAL DEPLOYMENT SUPPORT SYSTEM VOLUNTEER

Military & Family Life Support Center, Joint Base Anacostia-Bolling, Washington, DC

ADVOCATE: Provide assistance, support, and advocacy to service members and their families in preparation for deployments.

INTAKE ASSESSMENTS FOR FAMILY NEEDS: Assess family needs; provide information on referrals to appropriate resources; and follow procedures according to established standard operating procedures.

KEY ACCOMPLISHMENTS:

- RESEARCHER / DATABASE UPDATES: As a command representative assistant, gathered approximately 150 command/unit contacts (on and off base) and compiled the information into an Excel spreadsheet.
- Participated in PLANNING AND COORDINATING the Military & Family Support Center Military Appreciation Expo and Hiring event attended by 70+ employers and 400+ job seekers.
- Received the Presidential Gold Medal - for serving more than 500 volunteer hours (June, 2013)

STEP 1

Review the Federal Job Process

In Step 1:

Page

Use this worksheet to set your federal job search goals.

TARGET AGENCIES

What are your target agencies?

TARGET JOB TITLES AND SERIES

What is your current military job title?

How many years of specialized experience do you have?

Which federal job titles or series seem correct for you?

GRADE AND SALARY

What is your current military rank?

What is your current military salary?

What will be your target federal grade level?

What will your salary be, if you apply to a pay band agency?

DETAILS ABOUT YOUR FEDERAL JOB SEARCH

The following questions and answers will be helpful for writing your federal resume.

GEOGRAPHIC PREFERENCE
Where would you like to work and live?
You can list up to 4 locations.

TRAINING
Find your SMART transcript to list your relevant training, dates and classroom hours.

FEDERAL AGENCY PREFERENCE
Do you have a list of agencies that would be your preference?

EDUCATION
Do you have a Degree?
How many credit hours have you completed?

SALARY EXPECTATIONS
What is the LOWEST salary you can accept?

SPECIALIZED SKILLS AND KNOWLEDGE
What specialized knowledge and skills would you like to use in your next career?

JOB TITLES
List job titles of positions for which you would like to be considered.

COMPUTER SKILLS
List your computer skills.

CERTIFICATIONS
What are your certifications?

Match your MOS to GS interests online in just minutes!

Go to the Military to Federal Jobs Crosswalk: **www.mil2fedjobs.com**

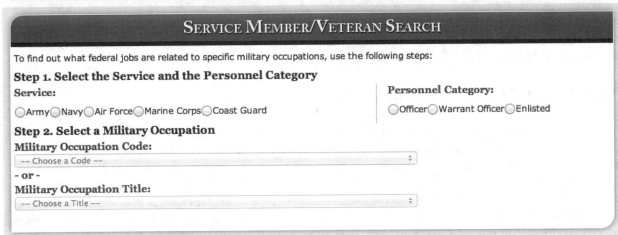

★ TYPES OF FEDERAL JOBS

Competitive Service Jobs

Competitive service jobs are under U.S. Office of Personnel Management's (OPM) jurisdiction and follow laws to ensure that applicants and employees receive fair and equal treatment in the hiring process. Selecting officials have broad authority to review more than one applicant source before determining the best-qualified candidate based on job-related criteria. Positions are open to the public. For positions lasting more than 120 days, vacancies must be announced and posted on USAJOBS, the federal government's central repository of job information. Veterans' preference rules are applied. Candidates are ranked and referred in order, i.e., highest scoring candidates or candidates in the highest quality group are referred first for selection. However, compensable disabled veterans "float" to the top, except for scientific and professional upper-level positions.

Excepted Service Jobs

Excepted service jobs are the jobs with agencies that set their own qualification requirements and are not subject to the appointment, pay, and classification rules in Title 5, United States Code. These agencies are able to be more flexible with recruitment incentives, salaries, promotions, and other personnel matters. They are also subject to veterans' preference. Positions may be in the excepted service by law, executive order, or action of OPM. Excepted service jobs are not required to be posted on USAJOBS. To learn about their job opportunities, you must go to the specific agency websites.

Direct Hire

Agencies use direct hiring when there is a shortage of qualified candidates, or when an agency has a critical hiring need, such as one caused by an emergency or unanticipated events, or changed mission requirements. Direct hire provides a quick way to hire individuals in the competitive service. Although it requires agencies to publicly post their vacancies on USAJOBS, they do not need to apply veterans' preference or rate and rank qualified candidates. Once a qualified candidate is found, agencies may offer the job on the spot and may appoint the candidate immediately. OPM has allowed government-wide use of direct hire for the following occupations: information technology management related to security; x-ray technicians; medical officers, nurses, and pharmacists; and positions involved in Iraqi reconstruction efforts requiring fluency in Arabic.

Pathways

Executive Order 13562, dated December 27, 2010, established a comprehensive structure to help the federal government be more competitive in recruiting and hiring talented individuals who are in school or who have recently received a degree. Student and recent graduate programs are to be consolidated into three clear program paths: internship program, recent graduate program, and the Presidential Management Fellows (PMF) program.

"Dual Status" Military Technicians

"Dual status" military technicians are federal civilian employees who are required to maintain military reserve status as a condition of their employment and are generally required to maintain membership in the National Guard as a condition of their employment. Military Technicians are assigned to civilian positions in administration and training of reserve component units, or in maintaining and repairing reserve component supplies and equipment. They are required to attend weekend drills and annual training with their reserve unit, and can be involuntarily ordered to active duty the same way as other members of the Selected Reserve. The Department of Defense, the Army, the Air Force, and the National Guard Bureau all oversee dual-status technicians.

Check the agencies of your choice.
View entire list at http://www.usa.gov/Agencies/Federal/All_Agencies/index.shtml.

Alphabetical list of organizations in the federal executive, legislative, and judicial branches

A

Administration for Children and Families
Administration on Aging (AOA)
Administration for Community Living
Administrative Office of the U.S. Courts
Advisory Council on Historic Preservation
Agency for Healthcare Research and Quality
Agency for International Development
Agency for Toxic Substances and Disease
    Registry
Agricultural Marketing Service
Agricultural Research Service
Air Force, Department of
AMTRAK (National Railroad Passenger
    Corporation)
Animal and Plant Health Inspection Service
Appalachian Regional Commission
Architect of the Capitol
Armed Forces Retirement Home
Arms Control and International Security,
    Under Secretary for
Army, Department of
Army Corps of Engineers (USACE)

B

Botanic Garden (USBG)
Broadcasting Board of Governors (BBG), (Voice
    of America, Radio/TV Marti, and more)
Bureau of Alcohol, Tobacco, Firearms, and
    Explosives (ATF)
Bureau of Economic Analysis
Bureau of Engraving and Printing
Bureau of Indian Affairs
Bureau of Industry and Security
Bureau of International Labor Affairs
Bureau of Labor Statistics
Bureau of Land Management

Bureau of Public Debt
Bureau of Reclamation
Bureau of Transportation Statistics

C

Census Bureau
Center for Nutrition Policy and Promotion
Centers for Disease Control and Prevention
    (CDC)
Centers for Medicare & Medicaid Services
Central Intelligence Agency (CIA)
Citizenship and Immigration Services Bureau
    (USCIS)
Civilian Radioactive Waste Management
Coast Guard (USCG)
Commission on Civil Rights
Community Oriented Policing Services
Community Planning and Development
Comptroller of the Currency, Office of the
Congressional Budget Office
Consumer Financial Protection Bureau
Consumer Product Safety Commission (CPSC)
Cooperative State Research, Education, and
    Extension Service
Corporation for National and Community
    Service
Council of Economic Advisers
Council on Environmental Quality
Court of Appeals for the Armed Forces
Court of Appeals for the Federal Circuit
Court of Appeals for Veterans Claims
Court of Federal Claims
Court of International Trade
Customs and Border Protection

D

Defense Advanced Research Projects Agency
Defense Commissary Agency
Defense Contract Audit Agency
Defense Contract Management Agency
Defense Finance and Accounting Service

Check the agencies of your choice.

Defense Information Systems Agency
Defense Intelligence Agency (DIA)
Defense Legal Services Agency
Defense Logistics Agency
Defense Nuclear Facilities Safety Board
Defense Security Cooperation Agency
Defense Security Service
Defense Threat Reduction Agency
Department of Agriculture (USDA)
Department of Commerce (DOC)
Department of Defense (DOD)
Department of Education (ED)
Department of Energy (DOE)
Department of Health and Human Services (HHS)
Department of Homeland Security (DHS)
Department of Housing and Urban Development (HUD)
Department of the Interior (DOI)
Department of Justice (DOJ)
Department of Labor (DOL)
Department of State (DOS)
Department of Transportation (DOT)
Department of the Treasury
Department of Veterans Affairs (VA)
Disability Employment Policy, Office of
Drug Enforcement Administration (DEA)

E

Economic and Statistics Administration
Economic, Business and Agricultural Affairs
Economic Development Administration
Economic Research Service
Elementary and Secondary Education, Office of
Employee Benefits Security Administration
Employment and Training Administration
Employment Standards Administration
Energy Efficiency and Renewable Energy
Energy Information Administration
Environmental Management
Environmental Protection Agency (EPA)

Equal Employment Opportunity Commission (EEOC)
Executive Office for Immigration Review

F

Fair Housing and Equal Opportunity, Office of
Faith-Based and Community Initiatives Office
Farm Service Agency (FSA)
Federal Aviation Administration
Federal Bureau of Investigation (FBI)
Federal Bureau of Prisons
Federal Communications Commission (FCC)
Federal Deposit Insurance Corporation (FDIC)
Federal Election Commission (FEC)
Federal Emergency Management Agency (FEMA)
Federal Financing Bank
Federal Highway Administration
Federal Housing Enterprise Oversight
Federal Housing Finance Board
Federal Judicial Center
Federal Labor Relations Authority
Federal Law Enforcement Training Center
Federal Mediation and Conciliation Service
Federal Motor Carrier Safety Administration
Federal Railroad Administration
Federal Reserve System
Federal Trade Commission (FTC)
Federal Transit Administration
Financial Management Service
Fish and Wildlife Service
Food and Drug Administration (FDA)
Food and Nutrition Service
Food Safety and Inspection Service
Foreign Agricultural Service
Forest Service
Fossil Energy

G

Government Accountability Office (GAO)
General Services Administration
Geological Survey (USGS)

Global Affairs
Government National Mortgage Association
Government Printing Office
Grain Inspection, Packers, and Stockyards
    Administration

H

Health Resources and Services Administration
Holocaust Memorial Museum
House of Representatives
House Office of Inspector General
House Office of the Clerk
House Organizations, Commissions, and Task
    Forces

I

Indian Health Service
Industrial College of the Armed Forces
Information Resource Management College
Institute of Museum and Library Services
Internal Revenue Service (IRS)
International Broadcasting Bureau (IBB)
International Trade Administration (ITA)

J

Joint Chiefs of Staff
Joint Forces Staff College
Judicial Circuit Courts of Appeal by Geographic
    Location and Circuit

L

Lead Hazard Control
Legal Services Corporation
Library of Congress

M

Marine Corps
Maritime Administration
Marketing and Regulatory Programs
Marshals Service

Merit Systems Protection Board
Mine Safety and Health Administration
Mineral Management Service
Minority Business Development Agency
Mint
Missile Defense Agency
Multifamily Housing Office

N

National Aeronautics and Space
    Administration (NASA)
National Agricultural Statistics Service
National Archives and Records Administration
    (NARA)
National Capital Planning Commission
National Cemetery Administration
National Communications System
National Council on Disability
National Credit Union Administration
National Defense University
National Drug Intelligence Center
National Endowment for the Arts
National Endowment for the Humanities
National Guard Bureau
National Highway Traffic Safety Administration
National Institute of Standards and Technology
    (NIST)
National Institutes of Health (NIH)
National Labor Relations Board
National Laboratories
National Marine Fisheries
National Mediation Board
National Nuclear Security Administration
National Oceanic and Atmospheric
    Administration (NOAA)
National Park Service
National Science Foundation
National Security Agency/Central Security
    Service
National Technical Information Service
National Telecommunications and Information
    Administration

STEP 1

Check the agencies of your choice.

National Transportation Safety Board (NTSB)
National War College
National Weather Service
Natural Resources Conservation Service
Navy, Department of the
Nuclear Energy, Science and Technology
Nuclear Regulatory Commission
Nuclear Waste Technical Review Board

O

Occupational Safety & Health Administration (OSHA)
Office of Government Ethics
Office of Management and Budget (OMB)
Office of National Drug Control Policy (ONDCP)
Office of Personnel Management
Office of Science and Technology Policy
Office of Special Counsel
Office of Thrift Supervision
Overseas Private Investment Corporation

P

Pardon Attorney Office
Parole Commission
Patent and Trademark Office
Peace Corps
Pension Benefit Guaranty Corporation
Policy Development and Research
Political Affairs
Postal Rate Commission
Postal Service (USPS)
Postsecondary Education, Office of
Power Marketing Administrations
Presidio Trust
Public Diplomacy and Public Affairs
Public and Indian Housing

R

Radio and TV Marti (Español)
Radio Free Asia (RFA)

Radio Free Europe/Radio Liberty (RFE/RL)
Railroad Retirement Board
Regulatory Information Service Center
Research and Special Programs Administration
Research, Education, and Economics
Risk Management Agency
Rural Business-Cooperative Service
Rural Development
Rural Housing Service
Rural Utilities Service

S

Science Office
Secret Service
Securities and Exchange Commission (SEC)
Selective Service System
Senate
Small Business Administration (SBA)
Smithsonian Institution
Social Security Administration (SSA)
Social Security Advisory Board
Special Education and Rehabilitative Services
Stennis Center for Public Service
Student Financial Assistance Programs
Substance Abuse and Mental Health Services Administration
Supreme Court of the United States
Surface Mining, Reclamation, and Enforcement
Surface Transportation Board

T

Tax Court
Technology Administration
Tennessee Valley Authority
Trade and Development Agency
Transportation Security Administration
Trustee Program

U

U.S. International Trade Commission

U.S. Mission to the United Nations
U.S. National Central Bureau – Interpol
U.S. Trade Representative
Unified Combatant Commands
Uniformed Services University of the Health
    Sciences

V

Veterans Benefits Administration
Veterans Employment and Training Service
Veterans Health Administration
Voice of America (VOA)

W

White House
White House Office of Administration
Women's Bureau

★ EXCEPTED SERVICE AGENCIES

These major excepted service departments and agencies do not post their vacancies on USAJOBS:

- Federal Reserve System, Board of Governors
- Central Intelligence Agency
- Defense Intelligence Agency
- U.S. Department of State
- Federal Bureau of Investigation
- General Accounting Office
- Agency for International Development
- National Security Agency
- U.S. Nuclear Regulatory Commission
- Postal Rates Commission
- Postal Service
- Tennessee Valley Authority
- United States Mission to the United Nations

Department of Veterans Affairs, Health Services and Research Administration:
Physicians, Dentists, Nurses, Nurse Anesthetists, Physicians' Assistants, Podiatrists, Optometrists, Expanded-function Dental Auxiliaries, Occupational Therapists, Pharmacists, Licensed Practical/Vocational Nurses, Physical Therapists and Certified/ Registered Respiratory Therapists.

Judicial Branch

Legislative Branch

Public International Organizations:
- International Monetary Fund
- Pan American Health Organization
- United Nations Children's Fund
- United Nations Development Program
- United Nations Institute
- United Nations Population Fund
- United Nations Secretariat
- World Bank, International Finance Corporation (IFC) and the Multilateral Investment Guarantee Agency (MIGA)

Find a link to the list of Excepted Service Agencies and Excepted Service Positions at:
www.resume-place.com/resources/useful-links/

Finding Your Job Titles

The government classifies jobs that share common characteristics into general work "groups" and specific "series." The occupations are generally divided into white-collar (General Schedule, or GS) and trades (Wage Grade, or WG) job groups. Use this section to identify possible job fits for your skills and interests.

If you are interested in more detailed information about the work performed by a particular job series, you can research the Position Classification Standards maintained by OPM. The standards and other classification documents are available on OPM's web site, at www.opm.gov/fedclass.

Keep in mind that the classification system explains how a job is assigned a title, occupational series, and grade, and explains the type and level of work done at each grade within an occupation. However, the classification standards do not address how an individual qualifies for a particular job or line of work. Information about qualifications is found in OPM's Qualifications Standards, at www.opm.gov/qualifications.

Carefully reading the qualifications requirements for various occupational series at the different grades will help you make realistic decisions about what jobs to pursue (title, series, and grade) and may save you from wasting time applying for jobs where you simply don't meet those requirements.

Find your target job titles from this listing of the HANDBOOK OF OCCUPATIONAL GROUPS AND FAMILIES, U.S. Office of Personnel Management Office of Classification, Washington, DC.

GS-000 – MISCELLANEOUS OCCUPATIONS GROUP (NOT ELSEWHERE CLASSIFIED)

This group includes all classes of positions the duties of which are to administer, supervise, or perform work, which cannot be included in other occupational groups either because the duties are unique, or because they are complex and come in part under various groups.

Series in this group are:
GS-006 - Correctional Institution Administration Series
GS-007 - Correctional Officer Series
GS-011 - Bond Sales Promotion Series
GS-018 - Safety and Occupational Health Management Series
GS-019 - Safety Technician Series
GS-020 - Community Planning Series
GS-021 - Community Planning Technician Series
GS-023 - Outdoor Recreation Planning Series
GS-025 - Park Ranger Series
GS-028 - Environmental Protection Specialist Series
GS-029 - Environmental Protection Assistant Series
GS-030 - Sports Specialist Series
GS-050 - Funeral Directing Series
GS-060 - Chaplain Series
GS-062 - Clothing Design Series
GS-072 - Fingerprint Identification Series
GS-080 - Security Administration Series
GS-081 - Fire Protection and Prevention Series
GS-082 - United States Marshal Series
GS-083 - Police Series
GS-084 - Nuclear Materials Courier Series
GS-085 - Security Guard Series
GS-086 - Security Clerical and Assistance Series
GS-090 - Guide Series
GS-095 - Foreign Law Specialist Series
GS-099 - General Student Trainee Series

GS-100 – SOCIAL SCIENCE, PSYCHOLOGY, AND WELFARE GROUP

This group includes all classes of positions the duties of which are to advise on, administer, supervise, or perform research or other professional and scientific work, subordinate technical work, or related clerical work in one or more of the social sciences; in psychology; in social work; in recreational activities; or in the administration of public welfare and insurance programs.

Series in this group are:
GS-101 - Social Science Series
GS-102 - Social Science Aid and Technician Series
GS-105 - Social Insurance Administration Series
GS-106 - Unemployment Insurance Series
GS-107 - Health Insurance Administration Series
GS-110 - Economist Series
GS-119 - Economics Assistant Series
GS-130 - Foreign Affairs Series
GS-131 - International Relations Series
GS-132 - Intelligence Series
GS-134 - Intelligence Aid and Clerk Series
GS-135 - Foreign Agricultural Affairs Series
GS-136 - International Cooperation Series
GS-140 - Manpower Research and Analysis Series
GS-142 - Manpower Development Series
GS-150 - Geography Series
GS-160 - Civil Rights Analysis Series
GS-170 - History Series
GS-180 - Psychology Series
GS-181 - Psychology Aid and Technician Series
GS-184 - Sociology Series
GS-185 - Social Work Series
GS-186 - Social Services Aid and Assistant Series
GS-187 - Social Services Series
GS-188 - Recreation Specialist Series
GS-189 - Recreation Aid and Assistant Series
GS-190 - General Anthropology Series
GS-193 - Archeology Series
GS-199 - Social Science Student Trainee Series

GS-200 – HUMAN RESOURCES MANAGEMENT GROUP

This group includes all classes of positions the duties of which are to advise on, administer, supervise, or perform work involved in the various phases of human resources management.

Series in this group are:
GS-201 - Human Resources Management Series
GS-203 - Human Resources Assistance Series
GS-241 - Mediation Series
GS-243 - Apprenticeship and Training Series
GS-244 - Labor Management Relations Examining Series
GS-260 - Equal Employment Opportunity Series
GS-299 - Human Resources Management Student Trainee Series

GS-300 – GENERAL ADMINISTRATIVE, CLERICAL, AND OFFICE SERVICES GROUP

This group includes all classes of positions the duties of which are to administer, supervise, or perform work involved in management analysis; stenography, typing, correspondence, and secretarial work; mail and file work; the operation of office appliances; the operation of communications equipment, use of codes and ciphers, and procurement of the most effective and efficient communications services; the operation of microform equipment, peripheral equipment, mail processing equipment, duplicating equipment, and copier/duplicating equipment; and other work of a general clerical and administrative nature.

Series in this group are:
GS-301 - Miscellaneous Administration and Program Series
GS-302 - Messenger Series
GS-303 - Miscellaneous Clerk and Assistant Series
GS-304 - Information Receptionist Series
GS-305 - Mail and File Series
GS-309 - Correspondence Clerk Series
GS-312 - Clerk-Stenographer and Reporter Series
GS-313 - Work Unit Supervising Series
GS-318 - Secretary Series
GS-319 - Closed Microphone Reporting Series
GS-322 - Clerk-Typist Series
GS-326 - Office Automation Clerical and Assistance Series
GS-332 - Computer Operation Series
GS-335 - Computer Clerk and Assistant Series
GS-340 - Program Management Series
GS-341 - Administrative Officer Series
GS-342 - Support Services Administration Series
GS-343 - Management and Program Analysis Series
GS-344 - Management and Program Clerical and Assistance Series
GS-346 - Logistics Management Series
GS-350 - Equipment Operator Series
GS-356 - Data Transcriber Series
GS-357 - Coding Series
GS-360 - Equal Opportunity Compliance Series
GS-361 - Equal Opportunity Assistance Series
GS-382 - Telephone Operating Series
GS-390 - Telecommunications Processing Series
GS-391 - Telecommunications Series
GS-392 - General Telecommunications Series
GS-394 - Communications Clerical Series
GS-399 - Administration and Office Support Student Trainee Series

GS-400 – NATURAL RESOURCES MANAGEMENT AND BIOLOGICAL SCIENCES GROUP

This group includes all classes of positions the duties of which are to advise on, administer, supervise, or perform research or other professional and scientific work or subordinate technical work in any of the fields of science concerned with living organisms, their distribution, characteristics, life processes, and adaptations and relations to the environment; the soil, its properties and distribution, and the living organisms growing in or on the soil, and the management, conservation, or utilization thereof for particular purposes or uses.

Series in this group are:
GS-401 - General Natural Resources Management and Biological Sciences Series
GS-403 - Microbiology Series
GS-404 - Biological Science Technician Series
GS-405 - Pharmacology Series
GS-408 - Ecology Series
GS-410 - Zoology Series
GS-413 - Physiology Series
GS-414 - Entomology Series

GS-415 - Toxicology Series
GS-421 - Plant Protection Technician Series
GS-430 - Botany Series
GS-434 - Plant Pathology Series
GS-435 - Plant Physiology Series
GS-437 - Horticulture Series
GS-440 - Genetics Series
GS-454 - Rangeland Management Series
GS-455 - Range Technician Series
GS-457 - Soil Conservation Series
GS-458 - Soil Conservation Technician Series
GS-459 - Irrigation System Operation Series
GS-460 - Forestry Series
GS-462 - Forestry Technician Series
GS-470 - Soil Science Series
GS-471 - Agronomy Series
GS-480 - Fish and Wildlife Administration Series
GS-482 - Fish Biology Series
GS-485 - Wildlife Refuge Management Series
GS-486 - Wildlife Biology Series
GS-487 - Animal Science Series
GS-499 - Biological Science Student Trainee Series

GS-500 – ACCOUNTING AND BUDGET GROUP

This group includes all classes of positions the duties of which are to advise on, administer, supervise, or perform professional, technical, or related clerical work of an accounting, budget administration, related financial management or similar nature.

Series in this group are:
GS-501 - Financial Administration and Program Series
GS-503 - Financial Clerical and Technician Series
GS-505 - Financial Management Series
GS-510 - Accounting Series
GS-511 - Auditing Series
GS-512 - Internal Revenue Agent Series
GS-525 - Accounting Technician Series
GS-526 - Tax Specialist Series
GS-530 - Cash Processing Series
GS-540 - Voucher Examining Series
GS-544 - Civilian Pay Series
GS-545 - Military Pay Series
GS-560 - Budget Analysis Series
GS-561 - Budget Clerical and Assistance Series
GS-592 - Tax Examining Series
GS-593 - Insurance Accounts Series
GS-599 - Financial Management Student Trainee Series

GS-600 – MEDICAL, HOSPITAL, DENTAL, AND PUBLIC HEALTH GROUP

This group includes all classes of positions the duties of which are to advise on, administer, supervise or perform research or other professional and scientific work, subordinate technical work, or related clerical work in the several branches of medicine, surgery, and dentistry or in related patient care services such as dietetics, nursing, occupational therapy, physical therapy, pharmacy, and others.

Series in this group are:
GS-601 - General Health Science Series
GS-602 - Medical Officer Series
GS-603 - Physician's Assistant Series
GS-610 - Nurse Series
GS-620 - Practical Nurse Series
GS-621 - Nursing Assistant Series
GS-622 - Medical Supply Aide and Technician Series
GS-625 - Autopsy Assistant Series
GS-630 - Dietitian and Nutritionist Series
GS-631 - Occupational Therapist Series
GS-633 - Physical Therapist Series
GS-635 - Kinesiotherapy Series
GS-636 - Rehabilitation Therapy Assistant Series
GS-637 - Manual Arts Therapist Series
GS-638 - Recreation/Creative Arts Therapist Series
GS-639 - Educational Therapist Series
GS-640 - Health Aid and Technician Series
GS-642 - Nuclear Medicine Technician Series
GS-644 - Medical Technologist Series
GS-645 - Medical Technician Series
GS-646 - Pathology Technician Series
GS-647 - Diagnostic Radiologic Technologist Series
GS-648 - Therapeutic Radiologic Technologist Series
GS-649 - Medical Instrument Technician Series
GS-650 - Medical Technical Assistant Series
GS-651 - Respiratory Therapist Series
GS-660 - Pharmacist Series
GS-661 - Pharmacy Technician Series
GS-662 - Optometrist Series
GS-664 - Restoration Technician Series
GS-665 - Speech Pathology and Audiology Series
GS-667 - Orthotist and Prosthetist Series
GS-668 - Podiatrist Series
GS-669 - Medical Records Administration Series
GS-670 - Health System Administration Series
GS-671 - Health System Specialist Series
GS-672 - Prosthetic Representative Series

GS-673 - Hospital Housekeeping Management Series
GS-675 - Medical Records Technician Series
GS-679 - Medical Support Assistance Series
GS-680 - Dental Officer Series
GS-681 - Dental Assistant Series
GS-682 - Dental Hygiene Series
GS-683 - Dental Laboratory Aid and Technician Series
GS-685 - Public Health Program Specialist Series
GS-688 - Sanitarian Series
GS-690 - Industrial Hygiene Series
GS-696 - Consumer Safety Series
GS-698 - Environmental Health Technician Series
GS-699 - Medical and Health Student Trainee Series

GS-700 - VETERINARY MEDICAL SCIENCE GROUP

This group includes positions that advise on, administer, supervise, or perform professional or technical support work in the various branches of veterinary medical science.

Series in this group are:
GS-701 - Veterinary Medical Science Series
GS-704 - Animal Health Technician Series
GS-799 - Veterinary Student Trainee Series

GS-800 – ENGINEERING AND ARCHITECTURE GROUP

This group includes all classes of positions the duties of which are to advise on, administer, supervise, or perform professional, scientific, or technical work concerned with engineering or architectural projects, facilities, structures, systems, processes, equipment, devices, materials or methods. Positions in this group require knowledge of the science or art, or both, by which materials, natural resources, and power are made useful.

Series in this group are:
GS-801 - General Engineering Series
GS-802 - Engineering Technician Series
GS-803 - Safety Engineering Series
GS-804 - Fire Protection Engineering Series
GS-806 - Materials Engineering Series
GS-807 - Landscape Architecture Series
GS-808 - Architecture Series
GS-809 - Construction Control Technical Series
GS-810 - Civil Engineering Series
GS-817 - Survey Technical Series

GS-819 - Environmental Engineering Series
GS-828 - Construction Analyst Series
GS-830 - Mechanical Engineering Series
GS-840 - Nuclear Engineering Series
GS-850 - Electrical Engineering Series
GS-854 - Computer Engineering Series
GS-855 - Electronics Engineering Series
GS-856 - Electronics Technical Series
GS-858 - Biomedical Engineering Series
GS-861 - Aerospace Engineering Series
GS-871 - Naval Architecture Series
GS-873 - Marine Survey Technical Series
GS-880 - Mining Engineering Series
GS-881 - Petroleum Engineering Series
GS-890 - Agricultural Engineering Series
GS-892 - Ceramic Engineering Series
GS-893 - Chemical Engineering Series
GS-894 - Welding Engineering Series
GS-895 - Industrial Engineering Technical Series
GS-896 - Industrial Engineering Series
GS-899 - Engineering and Architecture Student Trainee Series

GS-900 – LEGAL AND KINDRED GROUP

This group includes all positions that advise on, administer, supervise, or perform work of a legal or kindred nature.

Series in this group are:
GS-901 - General Legal and Kindred Administration Series
GS-904 - Law Clerk Series
GS-905 - General Attorney Series
GS-920 - Estate Tax Examining Series
GS-930 - Hearings and Appeals Series
GS-945 - Clerk of Court Series
GS-950 - Paralegal Specialist Series
GS-958 - Employee Benefits Law Series
GS-962 - Contact Representative Series
GS-963 - Legal Instruments Examining Series
GS-965 - Land Law Examining Series
GS-967 - Passport and Visa Examining Series
GS-986 - Legal Assistance Series
GS-987 - Tax Law Specialist Series
GS-991 - Workers' Compensation Claims Examining Series
GS-993 - Railroad Retirement Claims Examining Series

GS-996 - Veterans Claims Examining Series
GS-998 - Claims Assistance and Examining Series
GS-999 - Legal Occupations Student Trainee Series

GS-1000 – INFORMATION AND ARTS GROUP

This group includes positions which involve professional, artistic, technical, or clerical work in (1) the communication of information and ideas through verbal, visual, or pictorial means, (2) the collection, custody, presentation, display, and interpretation of art works, cultural objects, and other artifacts, or (3) a branch of fine or applied arts such as industrial design, interior design, or musical composition. Positions in this group require writing, editing, and language ability; artistic skill and ability; knowledge of foreign languages; the ability to evaluate and interpret informational and cultural materials; or the practical application of technical or esthetic principles combined with manual skill and dexterity; or related clerical skills.

Series in this group are:
GS-1001 - General Arts and Information Series
GS-1008 - Interior Design Series
GS-1010 - Exhibits Specialist Series
GS-1015 - Museum Curator Series
GS-1016 - Museum Specialist and Technician Series
GS-1020 - Illustrating Series
GS-1021 - Office Drafting Series
GS-1035 - Public Affairs Series
GS-1040 - Language Specialist Series
GS-1046 - Language Clerical Series
GS-1051 - Music Specialist Series
GS-1054 - Theater Specialist Series
GS-1056 - Art Specialist Series
GS-1060 - Photography Series
GS-1071 - Audiovisual Production Series
GS-1082 - Writing and Editing Series
GS-1083 - Technical Writing and Editing Series
GS-1084 - Visual Information Series
GS-1087 - Editorial Assistance Series
GS-1099 - Information and Arts Student Trainee Series

GS-1100 – BUSINESS AND INDUSTRY GROUP

This group includes all classes of positions the duties of which are to advise on, administer, supervise, or perform work pertaining to and requiring a knowledge of business and trade practices, characteristics and use of equipment, products, or property, or industrial production methods and processes, including the conduct of investigations and studies; the collection, analysis, and dissemination of information; the establishment and maintenance of contacts with industry and commerce; the provision of advisory services; the examination and appraisement of merchandise or property; and the administration of regulatory provisions and controls.

Series in this group are:
GS-1101 - General Business and Industry Series
GS-1102 - Contracting Series
GS-1103 - Industrial Property Management Series
GS-1104 - Property Disposal Series
GS-1105 - Purchasing Series
GS-1106 - Procurement Clerical and Technician Series
GS-1107 - Property Disposal Clerical and Technician Series
GS-1130 - Public Utilities Specialist Series
GS-1140 - Trade Specialist Series
GS-1144 - Commissary Management Series
GS-1145 - Agricultural Program Specialist Series
GS-1146 - Agricultural Marketing Series
GS-1147 - Agricultural Market Reporting Series
GS-1150 - Industrial Specialist Series
GS-1152 - Production Control Series
GS-1160 - Financial Analysis Series
GS-1163 - Insurance Examining Series
GS-1165 - Loan Specialist Series
GS-1169 - Internal Revenue Officer Series
GS-1170 - Realty Series
GS-1171 - Appraising Series
GS-1173 - Housing Management Series
GS-1176 - Building Management Series
GS-1199 - Business and Industry Student Trainee Series

GS-1200 – COPYRIGHT, PATENT, AND TRADEMARK GROUP

This group includes all classes of positions the duties of which are to advise on, administer, supervise, or perform professional scientific, technical, and legal work involved in the cataloging and registration of copyrights, in the classification and issuance of patents, in the registration of trademarks, in the prosecution of applications for patents before the Patent Office, and in the giving of advice to Government officials on patent matters.

Series in this group are:
GS-1202 - Patent Technician Series
GS-1210 - Copyright Series
GS-1220 - Patent Administration Series
GS-1221 - Patent Adviser Series
GS-1222 - Patent Attorney Series
GS-1223 - Patent Classifying Series
GS-1224 - Patent Examining Series
GS-1226 - Design Patent Examining Series
GS-1299 - Copyright and Patent Student Trainee Series

GS-1300 – PHYSICAL SCIENCES GROUP

This group includes all classes of positions the duties of which are to advise on, administer, supervise, or perform research or other professional and scientific work or subordinate technical work in any of the fields of science concerned with matter, energy, physical space, time, nature of physical measurement, and fundamental structural particles; and the nature of the physical environment.

Series in this group are:
GS-1301 - General Physical Science Series
GS-1306 - Health Physics Series
GS-1310 - Physics Series
GS-1311 - Physical Science Technician Series
GS-1313 - Geophysics Series
GS-1315 - Hydrology Series
GS-1316 - Hydrologic Technician Series
GS-1320 - Chemistry Series
GS-1321 - Metallurgy Series
GS-1330 - Astronomy and Space Science Series
GS-1340 - Meteorology Series
GS-1341 - Meteorological Technician Series
GS-1350 - Geology Series
GS-1360 - Oceanography Series
GS-1361 - Navigational Information Series
GS-1370 - Cartography Series
GS-1371 - Cartographic Technician Series
GS-1372 - Geodesy Series
GS-1373 - Land Surveying Series
GS-1374 - Geodetic Technician Series
GS-1380 - Forest Products Technology Series
GS-1382 - Food Technology Series

GS-1384 - Textile Technology Series
GS-1386 - Photographic Technology Series
GS-1397 - Document Analysis Series
GS-1399 - Physical Science Student Trainee Series

GS-1400 – LIBRARY AND ARCHIVES GROUP

This group includes all classes of positions the duties of which are to advise on, administer, supervise, or perform professional and scientific work or subordinate technical work in the various phases of library and archival science.

Series in this group are:
GS-1410 - Librarian Series
GS-1411 - Library Technician Series
GS-1412 - Technical Information Services Series
GS-1420 - Archivist Series
GS-1421 - Archives Technician Series
GS-1499 - Library and Archives Student Trainee Series

GS-1500 – MATHEMATICS AND STATISTICS GROUP

This group includes all classes of positions the duties of which are to advise on, administer, supervise, or perform professional and scientific work or related clerical work in basic mathematical principles, methods, procedures, or relationships, including the development and application of mathematical methods for the investigation and solution of problems; the development and application of statistical theory in the selection, collection, classification, adjustment, analysis, and interpretation of data; the development and application of mathematical, statistical, and financial principles to programs or problems involving life and property risks; and any other professional and scientific or related clerical work requiring primarily and mainly the understanding and use of mathematical theories, methods, and operations.

Series in this group are:
GS-1501 - General Mathematics and Statistics Series
GS-1510 - Actuarial Science Series
GS-1515 - Operations Research Series
GS-1520 - Mathematics Series
GS-1521 - Mathematics Technician Series
GS-1529 - Mathematical Statistics Series

GS-1530 - Statistics Series
GS-1531 - Statistical Assistant Series
GS-1540 - Cryptography Series
GS-1541 - Cryptanalysis Series
GS-1550 - Computer Science Series
GS-1599 - Mathematics and Statistics Student Trainee Series

GS-1600 – EQUIPMENT, FACILITIES, AND SERVICES GROUP

This group includes positions the duties of which are to advise on, manage, or provide instructions and information concerning the operation, maintenance, and use of equipment, shops, buildings, laundries, printing plants, power plants, cemeteries, or other government facilities, or other work involving services provided predominantly by persons in trades. Positions in this group require technical or managerial knowledge and ability, plus a practical knowledge of trades, crafts, or manual labor operations.

Series in this group are:
GS-1601 - Equipment, Facilities, and Services Series
GS-1603 - Equipment, Facilities, and Services Assistance Series
GS-1630 - Cemetery Administration Services Series
GS-1640 - Facility Operations Services Series
GS-1654 - Printing Services Series
GS-1658 - Laundry Operations Services Series
GS-1667 - Food Services Series
GS-1670 - Equipment Services Series
GS-1699 - Equipment, Facilities, and Services Student Trainee Series

GS-1700 – EDUCATION GROUP

This group includes positions that involve administering, managing, supervising, performing, or supporting education or training work when the paramount requirement of the position is knowledge of, or skill in, education, training, or instruction processes.

Series in this group are:
GS-1701 - General Education and Training Series
GS-1702 - Education and Training Technician Series
GS-1710 - Education and Vocational Training Series
GS-1712 - Training Instruction Series
GS-1715 - Vocational Rehabilitation Series

GS-1720 - Education Program Series
GS-1725 - Public Health Educator Series
GS-1730 - Education Research Series
GS-1740 - Education Services Series
GS-1750 - Instructional Systems Series
GS-1799 - Education Student Trainee Series

GS-1800 – INVESTIGATION GROUP

This group includes all classes of positions the duties of which are to advise on, administer, supervise, or perform investigation, inspection, or enforcement work primarily concerned with alleged or suspected offenses against the laws of the United States, or such work primarily concerned with determining compliance with laws and regulations.

Series in this group are:
GS-1801 - General Inspection, Investigation, and Compliance Series
GS-1802 - Compliance Inspection and Support Series
GS-1810 - General Investigating Series
GS-1811 - Criminal Investigating Series
GS-1812 - Game Law Enforcement Series
GS-1815 - Air Safety Investigating Series
GS-1816 - Immigration Inspection Series
GS-1822 - Mine Safety and Health Series
GS-1825 - Aviation Safety Series
GS-1831 - Securities Compliance Examining Series
GS-1850 - Agricultural Commodity Warehouse Examining Series
GS-1854 - Alcohol, Tobacco and Firearms Inspection Series
GS-1862 - Consumer Safety Inspection Series
GS-1863 - Food Inspection Series
GS-1864 - Public Health Quarantine Inspection Series
GS-1881 - Customs and Border Protection Interdiction Series
GS-1884 - Customs Patrol Officer Series
GS-1889 - Import Specialist Series
GS-1890 - Customs Inspection Series
GS-1894 - Customs Entry and Liquidating Series
GS-1895 - Customs and Border Protection Series
GS-1896 - Border Patrol Agent Series
GS-1897 - Customs Aid Series
GS-1899 - Investigation Student Trainee Series

GS-1900 – QUALITY ASSURANCE, INSPECTION, AND GRADING GROUP

This group includes all classes of positions the duties of which are advise on, supervise, or perform administrative or technical work primarily concerned with the quality assurance or inspection of material, facilities, and processes; or with the grading of commodities under official standards.

Series in this group are:

GS-1910 - Quality Assurance Series
GS-1980 - Agricultural Commodity Grading Series
GS-1981 - Agricultural Commodity Aid Series
GS-1999 - Quality Inspection Student Trainee Series

GS-2000 – SUPPLY GROUP

This group includes positions that involve work concerned with furnishing all types of supplies, equipment, material, property (except real estate), and certain services to components of the federal government, industrial, or other concerns under contract to the government, or receiving supplies from the federal government. Included are positions concerned with one or more aspects of supply activities from initial planning, including requirements analysis and determination, through acquisition, cataloging, storage, distribution, utilization to ultimate issues for consumption or disposal. The work requires a knowledge of one or more elements or parts of a supply system, and/or supply methods, policies, or procedures.

Series in this group are:

GS-2001 - General Supply Series
GS-2003 - Supply Program Management Series
GS-2005 - Supply Clerical and Technician Series
GS-2010 - Inventory Management Series
GS-2030 - Distribution Facilities and Storage Management Series
GS-2032 - Packaging Series
GS-2050 - Supply Cataloging Series
GS-2091 - Sales Store Clerical Series
GS-2099 - Supply Student Trainee Series

GS-2100 – TRANSPORTATION GROUP

This group includes all classes of positions the duties of which are to advise on, administer, supervise, or perform clerical, administrative, or technical work involved in the provision of transportation service to the government, the regulation of transportation utilities by the government, or the management of government-funded transportation programs, including transportation research and development projects.

Series in this group are:

GS-2101 - Transportation Specialist Series
GS-2102 - Transportation Clerk and Assistant Series
GS-2110 - Transportation Industry Analysis Series
GS-2121 - Railroad Safety Series
GS-2123 - Motor Carrier Safety Series
GS-2125 - Highway Safety Series
GS-2130 - Traffic Management Series
GS-2131 - Freight Rate Series
GS-2135 - Transportation Loss and Damage Claims Examining Series
GS-2144 - Cargo Scheduling Series
GS-2150 - Transportation Operations Series
GS-2151 - Dispatching Series
GS-2152 - Air Traffic Control Series
GS-2154 - Air Traffic Assistance Series
GS-2161 - Marine Cargo Series
GS-2181 - Aircraft Operation Series
GS-2183 - Air Navigation Series
GS-2185 - Aircrew Technician Series
Gs-2199 - Transportation Student Trainee Series

GS-2200 – INFORMATION TECHNOLOGY GROUP

Series in this group are:

GS-2210 - Information Technology Management Series
GS-2299 - Information Technology Student Trainee series

Trades, Craft, and Labor Positions
www.opm.gov/fedclass/html/fwseries.asp

Federal Classification and Job Grading Systems

Job Grading Standards for Trades, Craft, and Labor Positions

Job grading standards provide information used in determining the occupational series and title of jobs performing trades, craft, and labor work in the Federal Government. They also provide grading criteria for positions classified under the Federal Wage System (FWS).

If a series is not included in this list, we have not issued a specific job grading standard for that series. Documents on the Classifying Trades, Craft, and Labor Positions webpage provide series definitions and guidance on classifying jobs in series with no published standard.

Series	Occupational Group
2500	Wire Communications Equipment Installation and Maintenance Group
2600	Electronic Equipment Installation and Maintenance Group
2800	Electrical Installation and Maintenance Group
3100	Fabric and Leather Work Group
3300	Instrument Work Group
3400	Machine Tool Work Group
3500	General Services and Support Work Group
3600	Structural and Finishing Work Group
3700	Metal Processing Group
3800	Metal Work Group
3900	Motion Picture, Radio, Television, and Sound Equipment Operating Group
4100	Painting and Paperhanging Group
4200	Plumbing and Pipefitting Group
4300	Pliable Materials Work Group
4400	Printing Group
4600	Wood Work Group
4700	General Maintenance and Operations Work Group
4800	General Equipment Maintenance Group
5000	Plant and Animal Work Group
5200	Miscellaneous Occupations Group

Trades, Craft, and Labor Positions cont.

2500 Wire Communications Equipment Installation and Maintenance Group
2600 Electronic Equipment Installation and Maintenance Group
2800 Electrical Installation and Maintenance Group
3100 Fabric and Leather Work Group
3300 Instrument Work Group
3400 Machine Tool Work Group
3500 General Services and Support Work Group
3600 Structural and Finishing Work Group
3700 Metal Processing Group
3800 Metal Work Group
3900 Motion Picture, Radio, Television, and Sound Equipment Operating Group
4100 Painting and Paperhanging Group
4200 Plumbing and Pipefitting Group
4300 Pliable Materials Work Group
4400 Printing Group
4600 Wood Work Group
4700 General Maintenance and Operations Work Group
4800 General Equipment Maintenance Group
5000 Plant and Animal Work Group
5200 Miscellaneous Occupations Group
5300 Industrial Equipment Maintenance Group
5400 Industrial Equipment Operation Group
5700 Transportation/Mobile Equipment Operation Group
5800 Transportation/Mobile Equipment Maintenance Group
6500 Ammunition, Explosives, and Toxic Materials Work Group
6600 Armament Work Group
6900 Warehousing and Stock Handling Group
7000 Packing and Processing Group
7300 Laundry, Dry Cleaning, and Pressing Group
7400 Food Preparation and Serving Group
7600 Personal Services Group
8200 Fluid Systems Maintenance Group
8600 Engine Overhaul Group
8800 Aircraft Overhaul Group

Effective January 2014 – Annual Rates by Grade and Step

https://www.opm.gov/policy-data-oversight/pay-leave/salaries-wages/2014/general-schedule/

The General Schedule (GS) is a worldwide pay system that covers more than 1.5 million employees. The GS pay schedule has 15 grades and 10 steps in each grade covering more than 400 occupations. Pay varies by geographic location.

Grade	Step 1	Step 2	Step 3	Step 4	Step 5	Step 6	Step 7	Step 8	Step 9	Step 10	Within Grade
1	$ 17,981	$ 18,582	$ 19,180	$ 19,775	$ 20,373	$ 20,724	$ 21,315	$ 21,911	$ 21,934	$ 22,494	VARIES
2	20,217	20,698	21,367	21,934	22,179	22,831	23,483	24,135	24,787	25,439	VARIES
3	22,058	22,793	23,528	24,263	24,998	25,733	26,468	27,203	27,938	28,673	735
4	24,763	25,588	26,413	27,238	28,063	28,888	29,713	30,538	31,363	32,188	825
5	27,705	28,629	29,553	30,477	31,401	32,325	33,249	34,173	35,097	36,021	924
6	30,883	31,912	32,941	33,970	34,999	36,028	37,057	38,086	39,115	40,144	1,029
7	34,319	35,463	36,607	37,751	38,895	40,039	41,183	42,327	43,471	44,615	1,144
8	38,007	39,274	40,541	41,808	43,075	44,342	45,609	46,876	48,143	49,410	1,267
9	41,979	43,378	44,777	46,176	47,575	48,974	50,373	51,772	53,171	54,570	1,399
10	46,229	47,770	49,311	50,852	52,393	53,934	55,475	57,016	58,557	60,098	1,541
11	50,790	52,483	54,176	55,869	57,562	59,255	60,948	62,641	64,334	66,027	1,693
12	60,877	62,906	64,935	66,964	68,993	71,022	73,051	75,080	77,109	79,138	2,029
13	72,391	74,804	77,217	79,630	82,043	84,456	86,869	89,282	91,695	94,108	2,413
14	85,544	88,395	91,246	94,097	96,948	99,799	102,650	105,501	108,352	111,203	2,851
15	100,624	103,978	107,332	110,686	114,040	117,394	120,748	124,102	127,456	130,810	3,354

Now that we have covered the basic general schedule grade and pay system, we'll tell you that not every agency follows this pay system anymore. "Pay banding," which allows an organization to combine two or more grades into a wider "band," is an increasingly popular alternative to the traditional GS system. The "grade" information for jobs in agencies using pay banding will have a different look, and that look may be specific to a particular agency. Don't be surprised to see something as odd as ZP-1 or NO-2 in place of GS-5 or GS-7. Focus on the duties, the salary, whether you are qualified for the job, and whether you would like to have it. Remember, the federal government is large, and needs a way to increase flexibility of pay based on performance. Pay bands are its answer.

Example of Pay Band Salaries: Transportation Security Administration

http://www.tsa.gov/careers/pay-bands

Pay Band	Minimum	Maximum
A	$17,254	$25,227
B	$19,766	$28,831
C	$22,389	$33,636
D	$25,773	$38,660
E	$29,595	$44,447
F	$33,963	$50,999
G	$39,752	$61,592
H	$48,487	$75,134
I	$59,080	$91,624
J	$72,078	$111,718
K	$86,164	$133,559
L	$102,982	$157,100
M	$121,438	$157,100

The actual salary that the agency offers will be dependent on your qualifications. The general qualifications needed to receive that pay (and equivalent GS grade) is determined by the grade of the position. Please see the announcement for specific education and experience requirements for the position.

Salary Range (based on the 2014 pay schedule)	Qualifications Requirements
$20,200 – 36,000	High school with no experience (for GS-2) to one year of specialized experience at the GS-4 level, or four years of education beyond high school (for GS-5).
$27,700 – 44,600	Three years of general experience or one year of specialized experience or a bachelor's degree (for GS-5) or one year of graduate work or superior academic achievement as an undergraduate (for GS-7).
$41,900 – 66,000	Masters degree or equivalent or one year of specialized experience equal to GS-7 (for GS-9) or Ph.D. or equivalent or one year of specialized experience equal to GS-9 (for GS-11).
$60,800 – 130,800	One year of specialized experience equal to experience at the next lower grade (GS 12 through 15).

NOTE: All locality pay areas and definitions for 2014 are the same as those in effect in 2013.

Qualifying Based on Education Alone

GS-2:   High school graduation or equivalent (i.e., GED)

GS-3:   One year above high school

GS-4:   Two years above high school (or Associate's degree)

GS-5:   Bachelor's degree

GS 7:   One full year of graduate study or Bachelor's degree with superior academic achievement (GPA 2.95 or higher out of a possible 4.0)

GS-9:   Master's degree or equivalent such as J.D. or LL.B.

GS-11:   Ph.D.

NOTE: There are exceptions to this chart; there are occupations that will not accept education in lieu of experience.

Determining the government grade level based on your military rank is challenging. Here are some ways to determine the appropriate grade:

- **Salary:** Match the salary you are earning now against the OPM General Salary charts.

- **Specialized Experience:** Read USAJOBS announcements for the Specialized Experience required and see if you qualify for the grade level they are advertising.

- **Certification and Training:** Read job announcements and see if you have the specific certification and training required.

NOTE: The chart below is not an official federal government grade to military rank conversion chart. This chart was developed out of years of analyzing rank against the requirements of USAJOBS vacancy announcements for specific positions. Grade levels for these roles may differ based on an agency's organizational structure, geographical location, and/or size.

Federal Civilian Grade	Military Commissioned Officer	Military Warrant Officer	Military Enlisted
Assistants			Trainee/Assistants
GS-2, 3,4,5			E-2,3,4
6,7,8			E-5,6
Specialist/Technician	Junior Leaders / First-line Supervisors		Specialist/ First-line Supervisors
GS-7			E-3,4
9	O-1		E-5, E-7
11	2	WO-1	E-5, E-7
12	3	WO-1	E-7
Team Lead/ Section Leader *	Mid-level Leader/ Section Manager		Operations Supervisor/ Supervisor of First-line Supervisors
GS-12	O-3, 4	WO-2	E-7, 8
13	4	3	E-8
Supervisor/ Branch Chief *	Leader of Mid-Level Leaders /Manage Organizations		Superintendent/ Supervisor of Ops Supervisors
GS-13	O-4	WO-4	E-8, 9
14	5	5	E-9
Manager *	Senior Leader / Head of Organization		Senior Enl Advisor/ Career Field Manager
GS-14	O-5	WO-5	
15	6		

The human resources staffing specialist will detemine your qualifications for the position by looking at the following items in your federal resume. Qualification determinations are based on:

EDUCATION
➤ Major field of study
➤ # of years completed or # of semester hours completed
➤ GPA

TRAINING
➤ Related to job
➤ # of days or hours

EXPERIENCE
➤ Quality of experience
  • Directly related to the job or general nature of work
  • Complexity of assignments (what, for whom, why)
  • Decision-making authority or span of control
  • Knowledge, skills, and abilities used
➤ Length of experience
  • Full-time or part-time
  • # of hours per week

PATCO

Federal jobs are made up of the following basic categories, titles, and grades:

Professional – GS-5 through 15

Professional positions, such as chemists, accountants, doctors, social workers, and psychologists, have a positive educational requirement. They must be educated and certified by a board or institution.

Administrative – GS-5 through 15

These jobs usually have the title of Analyst or Specialist. Administrative jobs do not require a degree. You can qualify for an Administrative (Analyst or Specialist) position based on specialized experience, education, or both. Certain law enforcement positions are in this category: Special Agent, Border Patrol, Customs Inspector, Immigration Inspector.

Technical – GS-6 through 12

These jobs are the Technician or Assistant positions. Some job titles are Accounting Technicians or Assistants. There is no educational requirement. The main requirement is experience. The Federal Aviation Administration Electronics Technician can be classified as high as a GS-12. Bachelor's degree graduates can qualify for Technician or Assistant positions starting at GS-7 with superior academic achievement.

Clerical – GS-1 through 5

These jobs are Clerk positions. There is no degree requirement.
An Associate of Arts degree graduate will qualify for GS-3 or GS-4 positions.

Other

Law enforcement professionals (not special agents), including security guards, police, rangers, park rangers, and U.S. Marshals; blue collar and other professions not covered in other categories.

Are you or your spouse eligible for any special preferences or do you or your spouse belong to any special group of people? How about other members of your household?

Direct Hire

Agencies use direct hire authority when there is a shortage of qualified candidates (i.e., an agency is unable to identify qualified candidates despite extensive recruitment or extended announcement periods), or when an agency has a critical hiring need, such as an emergency or unanticipated event, or changed mission requirements. Its very nature allows agencies to forgo rating and ranking qualified candidates or applying veterans' preference.

Direct hire provides agencies a quick way to hire individuals in the competitive service. Positions filled through direct hire are posted on USAJOBS.

Certain agencies have direct hire authority for certain occupations. However, OPM allows the government-wide use of direct hire authority for the following occupations:

- Information technology management related to security
- X-ray technicians
- Medical officers, nurses, and pharmacists

Pathways

The Pathways Programs offer clear paths to Federal internships for students from high school through post-graduate school and to careers for recent graduates, and provide meaningful training and career development opportunities for individuals who are at the beginning of their Federal service. The Pathways program will include a/an:

- **Internship Program:** This program is for current students enrolled in a wide variety of educational institutions from high school to graduate level, with paid opportunities to work in agencies and explore Federal careers while still in school. Additional information about the Internship Program can be found at www.opm.gov/HiringReform/Pathways/program/interns/.

- **Recent Graduates Program:** This program is for individuals who have recently graduated from qualifying educational institutions or programs and seek a dynamic, career development program with training and mentorship. To be eligible, applicants must apply within two years of degree or certificate completion (except for veterans precluded from doing so due to their military service obligation, who will have up to six years to apply). Additional information about the Recent Graduates Program can be found at: www.opm.gov/HiringReform/Pathways/program/graduates/.

- **Presidential Management Fellows Program:** For more than three decades, the PMF Program has been the Federal government's premier leadership development program for advanced degree candidates. This program is now for individuals who have received a qualifying advanced degree within the preceding two years. For complete program information visit: www.pmf.gov.

Schedule A Hiring Program—Individuals with Disabilities, Including Veterans With a 30% or Greater Service Connected Disability

Abstracted from http://www.opm.gov/disability/mngr_3-13.asp

Important Note: The Schedule A appointment authorities were recently combined into one streamlined authority. The new regulation (5 CFR 213.3102(u)) also modernized the process in a number of significant ways.

What it provides: Federal agencies fill jobs two ways, competitively and noncompetitively. Persons with disabilities may apply for jobs filled either way. Jobs filled competitively are advertised through vacancy announcements. Jobs that are filled noncompetitively do not have to be advertised. Instead, a selecting official can select a person with a disability who has a Schedule A certification and is qualified for the job. People who are selected for jobs must meet the qualification requirements for the jobs and be able to perform the essential duties of the jobs with or without reasonable accommodation.

When it is used: People who are disabled and have a certification letter may apply for noncompetitive appointment through the Schedule A hiring authority. Applicants with certification letters may apply directly to agencies' Selective Placement Program Coordinators or their equivalent to be considered for jobs. Managers as well as individuals with disabilities may contact the agency's Selective Placement Program Coordinator or human resources office or their equivalent to obtain more information about sources for applicants with disabilities. A link to OPM's directory of Selective Placement Program Coordinators by agency is listed at the end of this section.

Who is eligible: The Federal Government has special appointing authorities for persons with disabilities. To be eligible for these noncompetitive, Schedule A appointments, a person must meet the definition for being disabled. The person must have an intellectual disability (mental retardation), severe physical disability, or psychiatric disability. In addition, the person must obtain a certification letter. Schedule A certifications may be written by a licensed medical professional, licensed vocational rehabilitation specialist, or any Government agency (federal, state, or District of Columbia) that issues or provides disability benefits. Each Agency is authorized to establish what documentation it will accept.

Agencies appointing under Schedule A Hiring Authority will determine whether the individual is likely to succeed in performing the duties of the job in the particular work environment. The agency may rely on the applicant's employment, education, or other relevant experience to do so. There may be cases in which the agency determines that it is necessary to observe the applicant on the job to assess whether he or she is able to perform the duties. In such cases, the agency may consider a temporary appointment of less than 90 days to determine job readiness and continued employment.

Service-connected disabled veterans may also be considered under special hiring authority for disabled veterans with disability rating of 30% or more from the Department of Veterans Affairs. Managers and supervisors can contact the agency's human resources office or Selective Placement Program Coordinator or their equivalent to obtain more information on appointment authorities.

Tips for Veterans Waiting for Disability Rating from Veterans Affairs

Qualifying Vets and Wounded Warriors in transition programs can apply for federal jobs through Schedule A as well, utilizing their 10-point preference. This may be an attractive option for those who are interested in applying for federal positions but have not yet received their VA disability rating.

Vets can apply for Schedule A certification or to get assistance through the local State's Vocational Rehabilitation Program (DORS in MD and throughout the country), even though they receive their services through the VA Vocational Rehabilitation & Employment program. The State Vocational Rehabilitation program can get the ball rolling and make connection(s) to the Veteran's VRE program.

Sample Schedule A Letter

To Whom It May Concern:

This letter serves as certification that [name of applicant] is an individual with a documented severe disability, identified by [name of physician/other certifying office] and can be considered for employment under the Schedule A hiring authority pursuant to 5 CFR 213.3102(u).

[name of applicant] also has certification of job readiness in an [ex: office setting, training, or other job setting] and is likely to succeed in performing the duties of the position for which he /she is seeking.

Thank you for your interest in considering this individual for employment.

You may contact me at ____.

For more information:

- *Selective Placement Program Coordinator (SPPC) Directory:*
  http://apps.opm.gov/sppc_directory/
- *OPM training on hiring people with disabilities:*
  http://golearn.gov/hiringreform/hpwd/index.htm

STEP 1

5 and 10 Point Veterans' Preferences:
7 Facts About How They Relate to Federal Applications

Veterans' Preference

By law, disabled veterans and veterans who served on active duty in the Armed Forces (during certain specified time periods or in military campaigns) are entitled to certain preferences over others in hiring for Executive branch competitive and excepted service appointments. Legislative and judicial branch positions are exempt unless the positions are in the competitive service or the agency has otherwise chosen to comply with Veterans' Preference provisions.

"Derived preference" is a method where the spouse or mother of a service-connected disabled veteran and the widow/widower or mother of a deceased wartime veteran may claim Veterans' Preference when the veteran is unable to use it. If eligibility criteria are met, the person will be given a 10 point preference.

Veterans' Preference does not guarantee a veteran a job. Rather, it gives eligible veterans a "preference" in certain appointments over other applicants.

FACT 1: FEDERAL RESUME AND VETERANS' PREFERENCE: When applying for Federal jobs, eligible veterans should claim preference on their application or resume. Applicants claiming 10-point preference must complete Standard Form (SF) 15, Application for 10-Point Veteran Preference, and submit the requested documentation.

DEPARTMENT OF THE NAVY

Job Title: ADMINISTRATIVE/TECHNICAL SPECIALIST
Department: Department of the Navy
Agency: Naval Sea Systems Command
Job Announcement Number: NW40080-04-10854624E782782D

SALARY RANGE:	$47,212.00 to $98,305.00 / Per Year
OPEN PERIOD:	Tuesday, April 01, 2014 to Thursday, April 10, 2014
SERIES & GRADE:	NT-0080-03/04
POSITION INFORMATION:	Full Time - Permanent
PROMOTION POTENTIAL:	04
DUTY LOCATIONS:	1 vacancy in the following location: Dahlgren, VA View Map
WHO MAY APPLY:	United States Citizens

FACT 2: U.S. CITIZEN USAJOBS ANNOUNCEMENTS – 10 POINT VETERANS RISE TO THE TOP OF THE LIST IN EACH CATEGORY: For the U.S. CITIZEN vacancy announcement on the previous page, if the agency uses Category Rating, those with Veterans' Preference will RISE TO THE TOP of each category. The names of preference eligibles with 10% or more disability will be listed in the highest category ahead of others (except for scientific and professional positions at the GS-9 level and higher).

FACT 3: STATUS USAJOBS ANNOUNCEMENTS – VETERAN APPLICATIONS ARE SCORED EQUALLY WITH ALL APPLICANTS. For the following STATUS announcement, Veteran's Preference will not apply (see "Who May Apply: status candidates"). "Status candidates" means current or former Federal civilian employees who have served at least 90 days after their competitive appointment. VEOA-eligible veterans may also apply and be considered under vacancy announcements limited to "status candidates". VEOA-eligibles are rated and ranked with other status candidates under the same assessment criteria; Veterans' Preference is not applied. If category rating is used, the selecting official may select any candidate from those who are among the best qualified.

Eighth U.S. Army

Job Title: Physical Security Specialist
Department: Department of the Army
Agency: Eighth U.S. Army
Job Announcement Number: FEEZ149442671085923

SALARY RANGE:	$50,790.00 to $66,027.00 / Per Year
OPEN PERIOD:	Wednesday, April 02, 2014 to Friday, April 11, 2014
SERIES & GRADE:	GS-0080-11
POSITION INFORMATION:	Full Time - Permanent
PROMOTION POTENTIAL:	11
DUTY LOCATIONS:	1 vacancy in the following location: Waegwan, South Korea View Map
WHO MAY APPLY:	Status Candidates (Merit Promotion and VEOA Eligibles)

5 and 10 Points for Veterans, and Derived Preference Eligibles

To receive preference, a veteran must have been discharged or released from active duty in the Armed Forces under honorable conditions. The veteran must also be eligible under one of the categories below:

5 Points are added to the rating of a veteran who served:

- During a war or
- During the period April 28, 1952 through July 1, 1955 or
- For more than 180 consecutive days, other than for training, any part of which occurred after January 31, 1955, and before October 15, 1976 or
- During the Gulf War from August 2, 1990, through January 2, 1992 or

- For more than 180 consecutive days, other than for training, any part of which occurred during the period beginning September 11, 2001, and ending on the date prescribed by Presidential proclamation or by law as the last day of Operation Iraqi Freedom

10 Points are added to the rating of a veteran who has served and:

- has a compensable service-connected disability rating of at least 10% but less than 30%
- has a compensable service-connected disability of 30% or more
- has a disability rating of less than 10% (receiving compensation, disability retirement benefits, or pension from the military or the VA but does not otherwise qualify in an earlier category)
- has received a Purple Heart

Note that the spouse, mother, or widow/widower claiming derived preference and meeting certain eligibility requirements will also have 10 points added to their rating.

Resource Note: If you are not sure of your preference eligibility, a good tool to assist you is the Veterans' Preference Advisor on the Department of Labor website.

Agency Procedures

Veterans' Preference is applied differently based on the method that the agency chooses to fill a competitive-service vacancy:

- **Category Rating.** Category Rating is the most prevalent ranking and selection procedure and applies to all competitive positions. It is intended to increase the number of eligible candidates from which a selecting official can choose while preserving Veterans' Preference rights. Applicants who meet the minimum qualification requirements for the position and whose Questionnaire/KSAs have been assessed are placed in one of two or more pre-defined quality categories instead of being ranked in numeric score order. Preference eligibles are placed ahead of non-preference eligibles within each quality category in which they are placed. There is an exception for veterans with greater than 10% disability—they "float" to placement at the top of the highest category (except for scientific or professional positions at the GS-9 level or higher). No preference points (5 or 10) are added to the preference eligibles' rating. An agency may not select a non-preference eligible if there is an eligible veteran in the same category, unless it received approval to pass over the preference eligible in accordance with law.

- **The "Rule of Three"**, under the traditional numeric rating procedure, required that selection be made from among the top 3 candidates with the highest number of application points. A candidate below the top 3 could not be selected unless a higher scoring applicant declined. However, the agency could not pass over a preference eligible to select a lower or same ranking non-preference eligible. A 2010 Presidential Memorandum ("Improving the Federal Recruitment and Hiring Process") requires agencies to use the category rating approach in place of the "rule of three" approach.

FACT 4: **FOR SCIENTIFIC AND PROFESSIONAL POSITIONS AT THE GS-9 LEVEL OR ABOVE,** applicants are added to the list in order of their ratings—including Veterans' Preference points. If category rating is used, 10% or more disabled vets are placed above non-preference eligibles within the same quality category for which they are assessed (rather than being automatically placed at the highest quality category).

FACT 5: **IMPORTANT NON-ELIGIBILITY FOR OFFICERS:** Unless disabled, retired officers above the rank of major or its equivalent will not be eligible for Veterans' Preference. Military Officers cannot claim 5 or 10 point preference, unless disabled.

FACT 6: **CLOSING DATES.** Generally, 10-point preference eligibles may file an application at any time. Any vet who is unable to file because of military service may also file after the closing date. It is advisable to contact the Agency's HR office for further information about specific positions.

Documentation

Vets must provide acceptable documents to establish eligibility for their preference. Acceptable documentation includes a DD-214 "Certificate of Release or Discharge from Active Duty," or a certification that you are expected to be honorably discharged or released from active duty not later than 120 days in the future. If you are claiming a 10-point preference, you will need to submit an SF-15 "Application for 10-point Veterans' Preference."

FACT 7: **SCHEDULE A HIRING IS IMPORTANT FOR VETERANS WITH DISABILITIES. Utilizing Schedule A Hiring Program if You Are Waiting for your Disability Rating.** Qualifying Vets and Wounded Warriors in transition programs can apply for federal jobs through Schedule A as well utilizing their 10-point preference. This may be attractive option for those who are interested in applying for federal positions but have not yet received their VA disability rating. See page 38 for additional information.

In addition to receiving preference in competitive appointments, veterans may also be considered for special noncompetitive appointments for which only they are eligible (those appointments are listed in the next section).

See also

- OPM Vet Guide: http://www.opm.gov/policy-data-oversight/veterans-services/vet-guide/
- OPM.Gov "Hiring Authorities": http://www.opm.gov/policy-data-oversight/hiring-authorities/competitive-hiring/#url=Category-Rating
- FedsHireVets: http://www.fedshirevets.gov/

Veterans Recruitment Appointment (VRA)
(Formerly Veterans Readjustment Appointment)

What it provides: VRA allows appointment of eligible veterans up to GS-11 or equivalent. Veterans are hired under excepted appointments to positions that are otherwise in the competitive service. After the individual satisfactorily completes two years of service, the veteran must be converted noncompetitively to a career or career-conditional appointment.

When it is used: VRA is used for filling entry-level to mid-level positions.

Who is eligible: VRA eligibility applies to the following veterans:
- Disabled veterans;
- Veterans who served on active duty in the Armed Forces during a war declared by Congress, or in a campaign or expedition for which a campaign badge has been authorized;
- Veterans who, while serving on active duty in the Armed Forces, participated in a military operation for which the Armed Forces Service Medal was awarded; and
- Veterans separated from active duty within three years.

30 Percent or More Disabled Veterans

What it provides: This authority enables a hiring manager to appoint an eligible candidate to any position for which he or she is qualified, without competition. Unlike the VRA, there's no grade-level limitation. Initial appointments are time-limited appointment of at least 60 days; however, the manager can noncompetitively convert the individual to permanent status at any time during the time-limited appointment.

When it is used: This authority is a good tool for filling positions at any grade level quickly.

Who is eligible: Eligibility applies to the following categories:
- Disabled veterans who were retired from active military service with a disability rating of 30 percent or more; and
- Disabled veterans rated by the Dept. of Veterans Affairs (VA) (within the preceding year) as having a compensable service-connected disability of 30% or more.

Veterans Employment Opportunities Act of 1998 (VEOA)

What it provides: This gives eligible veterans access to jobs otherwise available only to status employees. Veterans are not accorded preference as a factor but are allowed to compete for job opportunities that are not offered to other external candidates. A VEOA eligible who is selected will be given a career or career-conditional appointment.

When it is used: Agencies may appoint VEOA eligibles who have competed under agency merit promotion announcements when they are recruiting from outside their workforce.

Who is eligible: VEOA eligibility applies to the following categories of veterans:
- Preference eligibles; and
- Service personnel separated after three or more years of continuous active service performed under honorable conditions.

Many members of the armed forces start their civilian job search prior to discharge or release from active duty and do not have a DD-214 when applying for federal jobs. The Veterans Opportunity to Work (VOW) Act serves to ensure these individuals do not lose the opportunity to be considered for federal service (and awarded their veterans' preference entitlements if applicable) despite not having a DD-214 to submit along with their resumes. **In lieu of the DD-214, veterans and preference eligibles can submit other written documentation from the armed forces certifying that the service member is expected to be discharged or released from active duty service in the armed forces under honorable conditions not later than 120 days after the date the certification is signed.**

>> Request a "Statement of Service" from your Administrative Officer stating that you will be separating from the military on a certain date. This way you can apply for federal jobs before you receive your DD-214.

Excepted Service, Title 32 Dual Status Technician Jobs

"Dual status" military technicians are federal civilian employees who are required to maintain military reserve status as a condition of their employment. They are covered by both Title 5 (Civil Service employees) and Title 32 (Technician Act), and are generally required to maintain membership in the National Guard as a condition of their employment.

Military technicians are assigned to civilian positions in administration and training of reserve component units, or in maintaining and repairing reserve component supplies and equipment. They are required to attend weekend drills and annual training with their reserve unit, and can be involuntarily ordered to active duty the same way as other members of the Selected Reserve.

The Department of Defense, the Army, the Air Force, and the National Guard Bureau all oversee dual-status technicians. There are no dual status technicians in the Navy Reserve, Marine Corp Reserve and Coast Guard Reserve. The state Adjutant Generals are the designated employer of dual status military technicians.

Wounded Warrior Hiring

Wounded Warriors may be hired into the Federal government using any of several special appointing authorities granted by the Office of Personnel Management:

- 30 Percent or More Disabled Veterans (38 U.S.C. 4214 and Public Law 107-288)
- Veterans Recruitment Appointment (VRA) (5 U.S.C. 3301, 3302)
- Schedule A (persons with disabilities) (5 CFR 213.3102(u))

Definition

Wounded Warriors usually received injuries that required extensive hospitalization or multiple surgeries – such as loss of limb, loss of vision/blindness, spinal cord/paralysis, loss of hearing/deafness, severe burns, permanent disfigurement, traumatic brain injury, or post traumatic stress disorder. However, there is not one definition of "Wounded Warrior," and it is important to determine the definition that various programs may use. For example, to be eligible for the Department of Defense Outplacement Referral System (DORS) Program – a voluntary registration program for DoD jobs worldwide – a Wounded Warrior must have been an honorably discharged disabled veteran who has a compensable service-connected disability of 30 percent or more, "provided the disability resulted from injury or disease received in the line of duty as a direct result of armed conflict, or was caused by an instrumentality of war and was incurred in the line of duty during a period of armed conflict or war." Other agency programs may have additional criteria such as the injury was incurred in the line of duty after 9/10/2001.

Each branch of service operates Wounded Warrior programs designed to assist service members with their non-medical transition, including career resources. Enrollment and eligibility varies according to branch:

- Department of Defense's Operation Warfighter
- U.S Army Wounded Warrior Program (AW2)
- U.S. Navy Operation Safe Harbor
- U.S. Air Force Wounded Warrior Program (AFW2)
- U.S. Marine Corps Wounded Warrior Regiment
- U.S. Special Operations Command Care Coalition
- Military OneSource also provides Wounded Warrior specialty consultation

Other agencies and organizations providing transition resources include:

- Department of Veterans Affairs, Vocational Rehabilitation and Employment
- Department of Labor's Americas Heroes at Work
- Salute America's Heroes
- Soldier and Family Assistance Centers (at individual military bases)

Individual Federal agencies actively recruit severely wounded veterans at career fairs, military installations, medical centers, and transition workshops. Agencies provide Wounded Warriors the opportunity to apply for available positions without going through the standard competitive process.

Military Spouse Employment Preference (MSP)

What it provides: MSP provides priority in the employment selection process for military spouses who are relocating as a result of their military spouse's PCS. Spouse preference may be used for most vacant positions in DoD and applies only within the commuting area of the permanent duty station of the sponsor. Spouses may apply for MSP as early as 30 days prior to their reporting date at the new duty station.

When it is used: 1) Placements into competitive civil service vacancies in the 50 states, the Territories, the Possessions, and the District of Columbia; 2) Employment in foreign areas; 3) Nonappropriated Fund (NAF) employment; 4) Noncompetitive appointments in the civil service for spouses of certain members of the armed forces.

Who is eligible: This preference does not apply to separation or retirement moves. Spouses must be found best qualified for the position and may exercise preference no more than one time per permanent relocation of the sponsor. (If you accept a position with time limitations, i.e., temporary, term, intermittent, or NAF with flexible work schedules, you do not lose your MSP.)

Noncompetitive Appointment of Certain Military Spouses

What it provides: As of 9/11/09, federal agencies were granted the authority to hire "qualified" military spouses without going through the competitive process. Spouses can find out about job opportunities by going to USAJOBS or websites of specific agencies.

When it is used: The use of this authority is discretionary by federal agencies and the hiring managers. The authority is not limited to specific positions or grade levels, but spouses must meet the same requirements as other applicants, to include qualification requirements. Spouses are not provided any "hiring preference" nor does it create an entitlement to federal jobs over other qualified applicants. It is the applicant's responsibility to apply for a job and request consideration for employment under this authority as a military spouse.

Who is eligible:
- Spouses of service members serving on PCS for 180 days or more (provided the spouse relocates to the member's new permanent duty station)
- Spouses of retired service members (who retired under Chapter 61, Title 10, USA), with a disability rating of 100% at the time of retirement
- Spouses of former service members who retired or were released and have a 100% disability rating from the VA
- Un-remarried widows or widowers of armed forces members killed while serving on active duty.

DoD Military Spouse Preference Program (PPP) Program S

Overview

Military spouses who are relocating with their active duty U.S. Armed Forces spouse ("sponsor") as a result of permanent change of station (PCS) orders may be eligible for priority consideration/noncompetitive appointment to competitive service Department of Defense (DoD) positions in the continental U.S., territories and possessions. The term "Armed Forces" includes active duty Coast Guard and full-time National Guard. The Program does not apply to excepted service positions; positions in foreign overseas areas; positions filled through delegated examining or direct hire authorities; and certain other positions. To review Program specifics eligibility, see Chapter 14 of the Department of Defense Priority Placement Program (PPP) Handbook (http://www.cpms.osd.mil/Content/Documents/PPPHandbookAug2012(2).pdf).

Eligibility

Spouse preference eligibility begins 30 days prior to the sponsor's reporting date, and continues at the new duty station after relocation. Eligibility continues throughout the tour (with a requirement for re-registration after 12 months) until the spouse accepts or declines a continuing (permanent) appropriated fund position in the commuting area. There is a limit of one permanent appointment per PCS and the spouse must be immediately available for appointment. Positions must be within the geographic commuting area of the permanent duty station.

Until recently, most spouses gained their eligibility through their current or prior service as Federal career or career-conditional employees (or by virtue of certain other status). In 2008, Program S eligibility was expanded by Executive Order 13473 to include military spouses who were never Federal employees. The E.O. has the potential to facilitate the entry of more military spouses into the Federal Civil Service. The Executive Order applies to federal civilian service positions both within and outside of DoD. As a result, federal agencies may choose to exercise authority to noncompetitively hire under the E.O. The Order also applies more broadly to 2 other categories of military spouses. Executive Order 13473 is available at http://www.gpo.gov/fdsys/pkg/FR-2008-09-30/pdf/E8-23125.pdf.

Registration Process

Eligible spouses register in Program S at the Civilian Personal Advisory Center (CPAC) at the sponsor's prior or current duty station. It is important to bring a narrative resume and your most recent performance appraisal. You are also required to present the PCS orders showing authorization to accompany the sponsor to the new duty station, as well as proof of marriage (certificate of marriage or license). The Human Resources Specialists will assess which series and grades you are qualified for. If you do not have prior Federal Civilian Service, the HR Specialist will evaluate your experience, education, and training. It is essential that your resume substantiate your knowledge, skills, and abilities related to the series (1 or more) and grade(s) you are pursuing. See Chapter 10 of the PPP Handbook for information on "occupational codes".

Qualifying

Program S registrants do not need to meet the higher standard of being considered well-qualified to be considered for a position. They need only to meet the established minimum OPM Qualification Standard for the series/grade that they are registering for. If you are eligible for Program S, you must be considered if you are among the "best qualified," candidates. Under the DoD Priority Placement Program, eligible military spouses are given "Priority 3" status. "Priority 1" status applies to certain DoD employees scheduled for RIF separation; "Priority 2" status applies to certain employees scheduled for separation due to transfer or reassignment. Except for those having a higher Priority Preference Program priority, a better qualified military spouse "blocks the selection of other competitive candidates."

Why the Program S Military spouse PPP Program is a good idea!

"Good morning Kathryn! Any military spouse can get PPP if they apply for it within 30 days of a military move/PCS. All I had to do was call the CPAC office (civilian personnel advisory center) and make an appoint to "get" PPP. They evaluated my resume and gave me a GS-score BASED on my resume. Once I was in the system, I was told to apply on USAJOBS to whatever jobs I was good for. In the meantime, if they found a job on USAJOBS, they would "recommend" it to me. I would have a certain amount of time to apply; if I didn't at least apply, then I would be dropped from PPP. Once I accepted a job, I was pushed out of the PPP program. If it wasn't for your resume, I wouldn't have received a high GS score. If it wasn't for PPP, I wouldn't have gotten a job as fast as I did." -- Natalie Richardson

See Natalie Richardson's LinkedIn Resume on page 59.
See a true PPP-S Federal Resume with Option Codes for Dawn McCallem on page 105.

For more information: DOD PPP Handbook, Read Chapter 14 for Military Spouse PPP, Updated July 2011, www.cpms.osd.mil/care/care_ppp.aspx.

Derived Veterans' Preference

What it provides: By law, veterans who are disabled or who served on active duty in the Armed Forces during certain specified time periods or in military campaigns are entitled to preference over others in competitive external hiring. When a veteran is not able to use his or her federal employment preference, then the preference can essentially "pass on" to his or her spouse, widow, or mother. The eligible applicant receives an additional 10 points to a passing examination score or rating.

When it is used: This preference is based on service of a veteran who is not able to use the federal employment preference. This authority is not related to the MSP described above.

Who is eligible: Spouses, widows, widowers, or mothers of veterans who are unable to work as a result of their service-related disability or have died while on active duty. Both a mother and a spouse (including widow or widower) may be entitled to preference on the basis of the same veteran's service if they both meet the requirements. However, neither may receive preference if the veteran is living and is qualified for federal employment.

Veterans Have Great Tuition, Book, and Housing Benefits for Going to College

Post-9/11 GI Bill

For their service to America, veterans earn valuable education benefits. The Post-9/11 Veterans Educational Assistance Act, as amended (Post-9/11 GI Bill) is an education benefit program for individuals who served on active duty after September 10, 2001. For approved programs, eligible veterans may receive up to 36 months of education benefits, generally payable for 15 years following release from active duty.

Eligibility

Veterans may be eligible if they served at least 90 aggregate days on active duty after September 10, 2001, or were honorably discharged from active duty for a service-connected disability after serving 30 days. Service members can use the benefits while on active duty or after active duty. In order to be 100% eligible under the Post-9/11 GI Bill, a veteran generally must have served at least 36 months that were not obligated service time to any other benefit (such as attending one of the academies or the loan repayment program). An individual who was discharged due to service-connected disability after serving at for least 30 continuous days is also considered 100% eligible. Veterans are eligible to take advantage of benefits prior to the 36-month mark, but at lower rates. For example, after 90 days of service, the veteran would be eligible at 40%, and after 30 months eligible at 90%.

Brief Overview of Benefits

The Post-9/11 GI Bill provides financial benefits for undergraduate and graduate education to qualified veterans in the form of tuition and fees (paid directly to the school), a housing allowance, and up to a $1,000 book/supplies stipend. Other qualifying education and training programs under the GI Bill include: accredited non-college degree programs, correspondence training, apprenticeships, flight programs, licensing, certifications, and tutorial assistance. Note that benefits for specific programs may be subject to different reimbursement rates than those that apply to colleges and universities.

If a veteran is 100% eligible, the VA will pay the full amount of in-state tuition and fees at a public college or university. Tuition and fees at a private (or foreign) institution is subject to a national cap that changes annually. The cap is currently just below $19,200 (or actual tuition and fees, if lower). Private institutions in certain states are eligible for higher tuition reimbursement. To review specifics, see the Department of Veterans Affairs materials at http://www.benefits.va.gov/gibill/post911_gibill.asp.

> Example: A 100% eligible veteran, who has not yet received GI Bill education benefits, decides to attend a public or private university full time. The institution's tuition and fees are $15,000. Each year, the classes last 9 months, and the veteran enrolls full time for 4 school years -- 36 months of classes in total. The veteran may be eligible to receive more than $60,000 in covered tuition and fees (we assume that the costs will be reimbursed at a slightly higher rate each year). The applicable housing allowance and book/supply stipend is added to that amount.

Extra Funding Through the Yellow Ribbon Program (YRP)

Tuition and fee costs may exceed the national cap at private colleges and public institutions where the veteran is a nonresident. The Yellow Ribbon Program (YRP) supplements tuition and fees at participating institutions of higher learning with higher tuition and fees than the Post-9/11 GI Bill cap, without additional charges to the veteran's GI Bill entitlement. To be eligible for the Program, the veteran must be entitled to the maximum (100%) benefit level. Thousands of institutions have voluntarily entered into agreements with the Department of Veterans Affairs setting an institutional contribution. The VA matches that contribution. Schools set a limit on the contribution amount and the number of participants; benefits are generally awarded on a first-come, first-served basis.

> Example: The same 100% eligible veteran matriculates full time at a private university with tuition and fees totaling $31,000/year. The university participates in the Yellow Ribbon Program. Under the Post-9/11 GI Bill, the veteran will be eligible for benefits of just shy of $19,200 for tuition and fees, as well as the monthly housing allowance and annual book/supply stipend. The university's agreement with VA is to provide additional funding up to $5,000/year; the VA will match that amount. The veteran will receive an additional $10,000/year toward tuition and fees—tuition/fee benefits totaling $29,200/year through a combination of the Post-9/11 GI Bill and the YRP. Potentially, if the veteran continues to qualify and matriculates at the institution for 4 school years (36 months), he/she could receive well over $100,000 in tuition and fee benefits. Again, the housing allowance and book stipend will be added to that amount.

More information about the Yellow Ribbon Program is available by phone at the Department of Veterans Affairs, on the Department of Veterans Affairs website, or directly from the participating school. A list of Yellow Ribbon participating institutions is available at http://www.benefits.va.gov/gibill/yellow_ribbon/yrp_list_2013.asp.

Transferability

The GI Bill tuition benefit, or portions of it, can be assigned to a spouse or children. If a service member wants to transfer his or her benefit to a dependent, that service member must assign the benefit while still on active duty. Generally, a veteran must agree to serve four more years when transferring benefits. Transfer criteria is discussed in detail at http://www.benefits.va.gov/gibill/post911_transfer.asp.

More Information

Several other VA education and training programs offer various benefits to Veterans and their survivors and dependents. In addition to the VA website, service members and veterans can learn more about education benefits from their Military Base Education Office, and selected institutions' veteran's representatives (see http://gibill.va.gov). Excellent reference materials are also available at the Military.com education website at http://www.military.com/education.

STEP 2

Network – Who Do You Know?

Why Network?

The U.S. federal government employs nearly two million people in civilian jobs, making it the biggest employer in the country. Understandably, the hiring system can sometimes be complex and daunting. Networking is a great opportunity to learn about the federal hiring system. Other people, especially current and former federal employees, are often the best source of basic information and insider tips.

Who Do You Know and Why Is It Important?

Do you know a supervisor at an agency or a military base? It's possible that veterans could get hired by this supervisor. The Veterans Recruitment Act (VRA) offers special hiring programs for retiring and separating military (disabled or non-disabled). VRA gives supervisors the authority to make direct hires in the case of veterans, but even under direct hiring, the jobseeker must submit an application.

Contact List

Make a list of federal employee contacts and keep their information handy for networking.

Name of person:

Agency where he/she works:

Location:

Job title:

What does he/she do in the government?

One of the best places to learn about federal jobs, agencies, and opportunities is at a military career expo. On occasion, the federal human resources specialist may even bring along a few Direct Hire positions for government positions or internships. Have your resume ready to hand out. Your federal resume should feature your most relevant skills for easy reading and review by the Human Resources Recruiters. Also, practice the job fair script before you go.

Job Fair Script

Prepare your own job fair script here. Practice your script with a friend.

Hello, my name is: _____

Where are you from? _____

Military service: _____

_____

Recent activity: _____
What was involved in that? _____
What was the result of that activity? _____
What was your role? _____

What kind of job are you looking for? _____

_____

_____

What are your basic skills? _____

_____

_____

Where do you want to live now? _____

_____

_____

JOHN W. SMITH

Walter Reed Army Medical Center
Malogne House Bldg.20, Room 181
6900 Georgia Ave., NW
Washington, DC 20307
Phone: (202) 888-8888
Citizenship: United States of America

Permanent Address:
120 CR 546
Ripley, MS 21228
Email: johnsmith@yahoo.com

Veterans' Preference: 10-point, E-4, Mississippi Army National Guard, 2001 to present, Recipient of Purple Heart

SKILLS AND JOB OBJECTIVES:

Team Leader
Law Enforcement
Special Projects

Veteran's Benefits Counselor and Advocate
Emergency Management Coordination
Communications

PROFESSIONAL EXPERIENCE:

Active Duty, E-4. Completed one year of medical, rehabilitative recovery, reconditioning, counseling, and transition training in order to achieve wellness. Achieved a level of success to seek transition to civilian life. Walter Reed National Military Medical Center, Bethesda, MD, Jan. 2013 to Jan. 2014

Intern, Congressman Steven Palazzo – 12th Congressional District of Mississippi
2311 Rayburn House Office Building
Washington, DC 20515-2405
Supervisor: Harry Hoffman (202) 222-5555

August 2013 – January 2014
Salary: N/A
Supervisor may be contacted

While recuperating and completing physical therapy for injuries sustained as an escort Military Policeman in Iraqi Freedom, served as an Intern for Congressman Steven Palazzo.

- ADMINISTRATIVE ASSISTANT: Tasks included word processing, managing files and records, producing reports, designing forms, and other office procedures. Researched and produced reports on veteran's benefits activities. Corresponded with veterans.

- CONSTITUENT SERVICES: Provided customer and personal services to veterans concerning benefits and programs following injuries.

- VETERANS' BENEFITS RESEARCH: Researched TRICARE health insurance issues for national guardsmen and reservists while not on active duty. Advocated for veterans' benefits and provided information to representatives of the Department of Veterans' Affairs. Wrote summaries of veterans' problems and situations concerning processes and service treatment while being transferred from Walter Reed Army Medical Center to outlying regional centers.

JOHN W. SMITH, page two

Accomplishments:
- **Hurricane Sandy / Veterans Home Coordinator**: Coordinated the relocation of 100+ veterans from the Veteran's Memorial Home, Menlo Park, NJ to the U.S. Soldiers' and Airmen's Home located in Washington DC during the aftermath of Hurricane Sandy. Established phone card and clothing drives to ensure that each veteran had sufficient clothing and was able to contact family and friends concerning their whereabouts. Awarded the Humanitarian Service Medal and the Mississippi Emergency Service Medal for my actions.

Military Police, Mississippi Army National Guard

155th Separate Armored Brigade   July 2011 – August 2012
2924 HWY 51 South, Canton, MS 21042   Salary: $37,000/year
Supervisor: Capt. Stephen McCarthy (333) 888-8888 Supervisor may be contacted
- LEAD MILITARY PATROL AND LAW ENFORCEMENT: Lead military police patrol. Coordinate compound and work projects, preserve military control.
- TRAINER AND COORDINATOR: Train law enforcement personnel.
- TRAFFIC ACCIDENT INVESTIGATOR
- PHYSICAL SECURITY
- CIVIL DISTURBANCE AND RIOT CONTROL OPERATIONS

Manufacturing/Operations/Production

Ashley Furniture Factory   2008 - 2011
15900 State Highway 15 North, Ripley, MS 38663
- MANUFACTURING OPERATIONS MANAGEMENT
- CUSTOMER SERVICE AND PROBLEM-SOLVING

Equipment Operator/Supervisor

Pressmen Impact, Inc., New Haven, MS   2005 - 2008
- SUPERVISOR IN GOVERNMENT CONTRACTOR MANUFACTURING FIRM: Supervised custom impact extrusions serving aviation and military needs.
- TRAINED EQUIPMENT OPERATORS in safety and operations.
- EQUIPMENT OPERATIONS: Operated vehicles, forklifts and heavy machinery.

EDUCATION: Rydell High School, Rydell, Mississippi 37771, Graduated 2004
Mississippi Community College, Boonsboro, MS 38882
Major: Criminal Justice and Social Work, Semester Hours: 56 hours

LICENSE: Commercial Drivers License (Class A)

AWARDS: Army Commendation Medal, Iraq Campaign Medal, Global War on Terrorism, Expeditionary Medal, Purple Heart, Humanitarian Service Medal, Mississippi Emergency Service Medal, National Defense Service Medal, Army Service Ribbon, Armed Forces Reserve Medal

STEP 2

ANESHA T. GAFFNEY

PSC 999 Box 11, Rota, Spain, FPO, AE, 09634
666.666.6666
Email: anesha.gaffney@yahoo.com

Spouse Preference: Family Member of USN Active Duty
Eligible for Consideration under Executive Order 13473, September 11, 2009,
Non-competitive Appointment for Certain Military Spouses

SUMMARY OF SKILLS:

Instructor, Adult Educator
Program Developer and Coordinator
Mentor and Coach, Community Liaison
Administration, Writing and Computer Skills
Public Speaker and Speaking Coach

HIGHLIGHTS OF EXPERIENCE:

- *Family readiness and quality of life support:* career advisor, relocation counselor, and referrals for needed services for USN family members in Rota.
- *Provided adult education, instruction, and training* at University of West Florida, and increased operational readiness.
- *Coordinated and supervised* first Annual Northwest Florida Districts High School Speech Tournament.
- *Community liaison* establishing a network for the University of West Florida and N.A.S. Pensacola.
- *President's Award for Leadership and Diversity*, Univ. of W. FL (2008).
- *Proficient in Microsoft Office programs,* Windows Movie Maker, Final Cut Pro, and iMovie. *Typing Speed 60 wpm.*

WORK EXPERIENCE:

Fleet and Family Support Center, US Navy, Rota, Spain
Volunteer, 8/2010 – Present, 20 hours per week

• INFORMATION AND REFERRAL: Identified and clarified issues or concerns and determined appropriate referral services for military members, retirees, and family members. Ensured customer service and satisfaction.
• CUSTOMER SERVICE: Primary contact for department and ensured and delivered services to customers including educating clients on Relocation Services and Career Resource Development.
• MARKETING: Gathered data for Fleet and Family Support Center and updated information for department calendar and for NAVSTA Rota advertisement.
• DATA GATHERING: Utilized Microsoft Office software to compile and report information and statistics for use at the installation.

University of West Florida, Tampa, FL

Graduate Assistant Coach, 8/2008 to 5/2010, 30 hours per week

• INSTRUCTOR AND COACH. Designed training structure and determined appropriate alternative routes to more effective coaching techniques.
-- Over 5,000 hours of coaching students in effective writing and presentation skills.

• RECRUITER. Made recommendations for University of West Florida Forensics Team. Community liaison for team.
-- Created promotional DVDs; coordinated external events on campus to recruit on-campus students. Coordinated with Director of Forensics with national and regional travel plans for approximately 10 students.

EDUCATION:

Master of Science, Public Administration, 2010
University of West Florida, Pensacola, FL
Financial Management, Public Budgeting
Public Service Human Resources Management
Conflict Management & Resolution, Marketing Management

Bachelor of Arts in Organizational Communications, 2008
University of West Florida, Pensacola, FL

- Leadership Communications (Project Car-A-Van) - raised funds to purchase 15-passenger van for Ronald McDonald House of Northwest Florida (2006).
- Health Communications (Project KidCare) - Worked with Florida KidCare to raise awareness of medical insurance to families of lower socioeconomic status (2008).

HONORS

- Outstanding Graduate Student Award, University of West Florida (2010) Recipient of Letter of Appreciation from Commanding Officer for Volunteer Service, N.A.S. Pensacola (2009)
- President's Award for Leadership and Diversity, University of West Florida (2008)
- Four-time National Finalist: 2008 Pi Kappa Delta National Speech and Debate Championship Finalist (2005-2008)
- Top 24 collegiate speaker in the US in multiple categories, National Forensic Association (2008)
- Volunteer Shining Star Award, Ronald McDonald House of Northwest Florida (2007)

Life is about relationships, and LinkedIn has opened the door to help build more relationships worldwide.

LinkedIn, with 250 million professionals in its network, is THE business channel for recruiting. However, it is also so much more. LinkedIn provides an opportunity to build a worldwide network of professionals who can assist you with your career. Not only does it work for military to civilian transitions, it also works within the military framework where military to military assignments are concerned. Many military members have made connections for their next military assignment with another military professional using LinkedIn. LinkedIn can be regarded as a marvelous "networking" tool, though it should not be used as a substitute for good old fashioned relationship building.

LinkedIn is a great tool for military spouses for PCS moves. Before LinkedIn, it was very difficult to build a professional network outside of your current assignment. With the worldwide network that LinkedIn provides, military spouses are now able to build a professional network online.

Whether it is a short notice PCS move, a change in PCS orders, or a normal PCS rotation, or even in the case of a service member's extended or remote tours of duty (deployment etc.), military spouses can build strong professional networks via LinkedIn.

Fast updates to your network (and their network) for frequent moves! With the ability of LinkedIn to share the same message with 50 of your contacts at a click of the button, it will not take long to inform your entire contact list of any changes in your business and professional circumstance. Each of your contacts will also have other contacts who will be able to refer you to positions, whether you are simply looking for a change or moving due to a military assignment.

Employers expect to find professionals on LinkedIn. Many of our clients report that their LinkedIn profile was reviewed prior to their interview by the interviewers. This situation works fabulously both ways. The interviewer will have a great impression of you if you have done your work on LinkedIn, and you can research the interviewer prior to your interview.

The LinkedIn resume for Natalie Richardson on the facing page was developed based on her federal resume. We added an exciting profile with her most outstanding skills. LinkedIn is a professional place where you can post a photograph and introduce your strengths, mission, and career history to an employer or network. You can even ask for recommendations from your best customers or team members who will write about your strengths and accomplishments.

Did You Know?

Business professionals and human resources managers use LinkedIn to check out potential job candidates. Individuals with more than 20 connections are **34 times** more likely to be approached with a job opportunity.

Natalie Richardson

Public Affairs Specialist at US Navy Reserves

Chesapeake, Virginia | Public Relations and Communications

2nd

Previous   Sendmilitarycoupons.com, Self-Promotions Biz Cards, Chiropractic Health-Care

Education   Devry University-California

Connect   **Send Natalie InMail** ▼

2
connections

 www.linkedin.com/in/nbrichardson

Background

 Summary

Is your company looking for a Public Relations Specialist experienced in Military Affairs? Do you need somebody who can shape the message of your organization to reach new audiences? I am your public affairs specialist!

"Send It To Your Sweetie" Program took off! I founded and ran a successful marketing program for military families who had loved ones in Iraq. This unique program offered free services to military families with members in Iraq for shipping, phone messages, and personal delivery of gifts for their loved ones. I also liaised with base command to ensure all regulations and policies were met.

My expertise includes:
- Entrepreneurial spirit and creativity
- Communications and liaison
- Writing and marketing strategies
- Community relations
- Caring for military families and veterans

Experience

Public Affairs Specialist

US Navy Reserves

February 2012 – Present (2 years 3 months) | Hampton, Virginia Area

Successfully landed excellent position as GS-9 Public Affairs Specialist in charge of all advertising for recruiting program.

STEP 2

PARTNER/MANAGER

Sendmilitarycoupons.com

September 2010 – February 2011 (6 months) | San Diego, CA

MARKETING PROGRAM FOR MILITARY FAMILIES WITH FAMILY MEMBER IN IRAQ. Developed, owned, managed and operated business that sold marketing contracts to local businesses. Marketed "Send It To Your Sweetie" program targeting free services to military families with members in Iraq for shipping, phone messages, and personal delivery of gifts for their loved ones. Met with base command to ensure all regulations and policies were met.

• Accomplishment: Conceptualized a successful program for family members to send gifts and messages to military personnel. More than 2,500 messages were sent through this program in just 6 months. Sold business in less than 6 months for a substantial profit.

COMMUNICATIONS. Wrote business plan and developed all aspects of advertising and marketing. Performed cold calls on business customers and followed up with written proposals. Created and delivered PowerPoint presentations to groups of various sizes. Organized and prepared mailings to families and businesses.

WEBSITE DESIGN: Designed website and prepared spreadsheet to track monthly views and clicks. Due to volume of business, interviewed and hired 3 contractors to assist with billing, designing ads, and updating website.

MANAGER

Self-Promotions Biz Cards

June 2005 – July 2009 (4 years 2 months) | 29 Palms, CA

CREATIVE PRODUCTION: Sold and created full-color, personalized business cards to small businesses. Planned and organized work; efficiently and effectively processed the sale, design, ordering and delivery of product. Ensured quality control and timeliness for re-orders.

• Established a successful in-home business with local producers of business cards. Contracted with more than 15 vendors and tracked orders for more than 200 customers in two years. Efficiently set up and managed own schedule and schedule for automatic reordering.

CUSTOMER SERVICES: Provided administrative support to customers and vendors. Prepared and sent invoices, collected. Conducted all aspects of accounting.

COMMUNICATION: Corresponded with clients by email and phone, ensured correct grammar, spelling and format. Made cold calls on small businesses – utilized interpersonal skills to develop customer base of 300 businesses within 6 months.

COMPUTER SKILLS: Utilized typing speed of 45 wpm, Microsoft Suite programs for reports and communication, as well as Photoshop, Illustrator and Corel software to design cards.

Demonstrated strong customer services skills; multi-tasked and worked under pressure and constant deadlines. Maintained customer relations; photographed clients and worked with customers to achieve their desired customized product.

PUBLIC RELATIONS

Chiropractic Health-Care

February 2004 – January 2005 (1 year) | San Diego, CA

BUSINESS DEVELOPMENT AND COMMUNICATIONS: Represented chiropractic clinic public relations, made new business contacts, mended old contacts. Developed lasting business relationships with store managers, district managers and their assistants both inside and outside the office. Scheduled health screenings involving blood pressure, glucose and cholesterol testing. Ensured excellent service. Successfully increased patient roster by an average of 5 new patients per week.

STORE MANAGER

Lulu's Boutique

April 2002 – February 2004 (1 year 11 months) | Los Angeles, CA

ADMINISTRATION: Performed office and store administration including management of files and official records, training, payroll and reporting. Communicated effectively orally and in writing. Developed, wrote, standardized and regulated customer service procedures, policies and systems.

COMMUNICATIONS: Communicated with diverse customers, vendors, management to increase sales and resolve problems. Greeted and assisted customers with special requests. Trained staff to deliver excellent customer service.

COMPUTER SKILLS: Utilized computer skills to design website and regulate maintenance for user effectiveness. Used Microsoft Word for correspondence and Excel for reports. Ensured accuracy, correct grammar, spelling, punctuation and syntax.

MANAGED STAFF AND BUDGET: Planned and organized work for sales staff; managed budgeting for cost effective sales planning, directed all tasks and aspects of controlling, maintaining and rotating inventory. Designed store layout and product presentations.

MARKETING SOLUTIONS: Gathered pertinent data, and recognized solutions to initiate and conduct successful storewide marketing campaigns. Controlled and minimized expenses to maximize profit through selected business improvements.

 Languages

Spanish   **French**

 Skills & Endorsements

Microsoft Office

Spanish

French

Graphic Design

 Education

Devry University-California

2000 – 2002

Activities and Societies: Marketing and Business Courses

The best way to understand where you fit in government is to search for jobs that fit your experience and interests. Federal vacancy announcements (job advertisements) contain all of the information you need to compare your background to the position requirements.

Types of Federal Job Openings

When you are searching for a federal job, it is helpful to know that there are generally four types of vacancies.

Competitive Service jobs are posted on USAJOBS.

Excepted Service Agencies are not required to post jobs on USAJOBS.

Excepted Service Positions are jobs which also do not have to be posted on USAJOBS.

Find a link to the list of Excepted Service Agencies and Excepted Service Positions at www.resume-place.com/resources/useful-links/.

Agencies can also make Direct Hires for critical need positions or in situations where there is a shortage of candidates. All direct hire authority positions must be posted on USAJOBS. For a list of current direct hire authority positions, visit www.opm.gov/hr_practitioners/lawsregulations/appointingauthorities/index.asp#directhire.

Types of Federal Appointments

Competitive

- Jobs are posted publicly and candidates compete with each other

Non-competitive

- Jobs are not required to be posted publicly
- Jobs may be critical or high-need
- People with certain preferences can get jobs directly, without competing

About 5,000 job announcements are posted on USAJOBS (www.usajobs.gov) every day! Learn how to search effectively and efficiently to locate the vacancy announcements that are best for you.

Search by Keyword and Geographic Location

This is the easiest search to perform and will return a large number of results.

- Go to the USAJOBS home page.

- Enter keywords and geographic location.

- Try to use keywords specific to your unique skill set or the correct job title in quotation marks.

USAJOBS Advanced Search

You can quickly and efficiently refine your USAJOBS job announcement search using the Advanced Search function. For example:

- Search for federal jobs with certain grade or salary level in a certain geographic region
- Search for all jobs worldwide for a certain agency
- Search for all jobs within a certain occupational series or keyword either worldwide or within a certain geographic location

For the above question "Who May Apply":
- If you are a veteran, Schedule A or any of the choices above, answer YES.
- If you have no special hiring program consideration, answer NO.

Follow the Directions!

The following items are the most important elements of a vacancy announcement. Be sure to study each of these items on every announcement so that you follow the directions successfully.

Closing Date — The Closing Dates are Getting Closer!

Due to the number of applications, many closing dates allow only 5 to 7 days. Get your federal resume written ahead of the perfect USAJOBS announcement. If an announcement reads, "Open Continuous" or "Inventory Building", or has a closing date that is twelve months away, then this announcement is a database-building announcement. Try to submit one day early, so you have all of your documents and in case there is a complication with the submission. NOTE: Disabled veterans CAN apply to positions after the closing date, but it is better to submit on time.

Knowledge, Skills, and Abilities are KEYWORDS!

Read the announcement to see if they list KSAs. If KSAs are listed, you will need to cover them in the federal resume. The Outline Format federal resume style in this book is perfect for featuring KSAs in the resume. Use the KSAs for headlines in your work experience descriptions. Then add an accomplishment that will demonstrate your KSAs.

Questionnaires — Beware, this is a TEST! You need 85 to 90!

Almost all USAJOBS announcements require completion of a questionnaire. In these "self-assessment questionnaires," you choose your level of skill and experience for each question. Do not deflate your answers. Give yourself all the credit that you can with your answers. Your Questionnaire score must be 85 to 90 in order to get Best Qualified. PLUS ... Your resume must match your answers to the questions. Human resources will compare the questionnaire to your resume.

Duties

The description of duties will be written based on the actual position description. The write-up will include "keywords" that should be included in a federal resume.

Qualifications

Are you qualified? Read the qualifications to determine if you have the general and specialized qualifications. If the announcement states one year, that means 52 weeks, 40 hours per week.

How to Apply

Carefully read the "how to apply" instructions as they will differ from agency to agency. The usual application includes a resume, KSAs (if requested separately), last performance evaluation (if possible), DD-214 (if you were in the military), and transcripts (if requested or if you are applying based on education).

STEP 3

SPECIALIZED EXPERIENCE

is usually defined as experience that is similar to the position in the announcement. This section of an announcement is very important for federal resume writers. The announcement will often say, "Examples include," then suggest examples. Your federal resume MUST cover this specialized experience somewhere in the work experience. Your example does NOT have to be from your most recent position; it can be from any point in your work history, but preferably from the last 10 years.

Job Title: RANGE OPERATIONS SPECIALIST
Department: Department of the Army
Agency: Army National Guard Units (Title 32)
Job Announcement Number: T14-236

SALARY RANGE:	$54,035.00 to $70,243.00 / Per Year
OPEN PERIOD:	Tuesday, March 18, 2014 to Friday, April 18, 2014
SERIES & GRADE:	GS-0301-09
POSITION INFORMATION:	Full Time - Excepted Service Permanent
DUTY LOCATIONS:	1 vacancy in the following location: Camp Smith, NY View Map
WHO MAY APPLY:	New York Army National Guard membership required (See Announcement)
SECURITY CLEARANCE:	Not Applicable
SUPERVISORY STATUS:	No
JOB SUMMARY:	

QUALIFICATIONS REQUIRED: Back to top

In order to meet the minimum qualifications for this RANGE OPERATIONS SPECIALIST position, you must meet the following criteria.

GENERAL EXPERIENCE:

Experience, education, or training which provided a general knowledge of principles of organization, management, and administration. Experience using computer and automation systems.

SPECIALIZED EXPERIENCE:

Must have at least 24 months experience, education or training in any position that required compiling reports, letters, memoranda, etc., and required person-to-person contacts to convey information. Applicants must have experience providing technical guidance and assistance in the type of work or in comparable work of the position to be filled. Applicants must have a thorough knowledge and understanding of administrative procedures and practices of management. Experience developing administrative procedures.

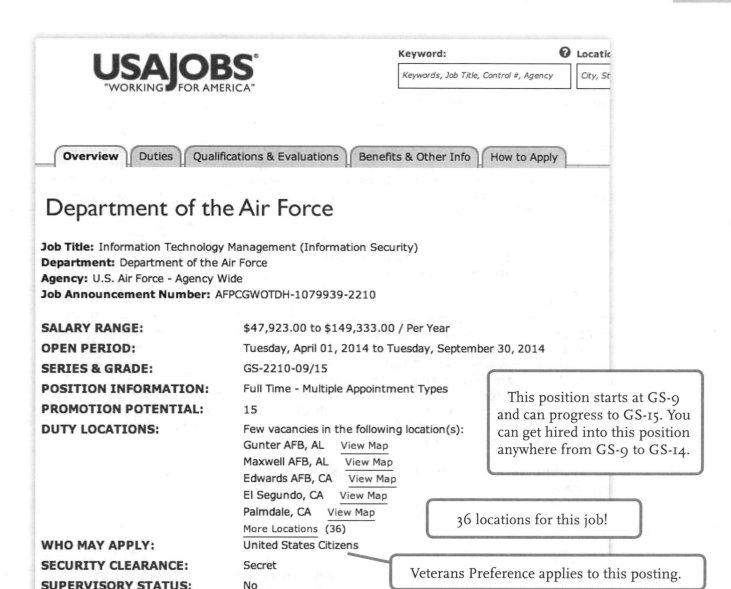

USAJOBS®
"WORKING FOR AMERICA"

Keyword:
Keywords, Job Title, Control #, Agency

❓ Locatio
City, St

| Overview | Duties | Qualifications & Evaluations | Benefits & Other Info | How to Apply |

Department of the Air Force

Job Title: Information Technology Management (Information Security)
Department: Department of the Air Force
Agency: U.S. Air Force - Agency Wide
Job Announcement Number: AFPCGWOTDH-1079939-2210

SALARY RANGE:	$47,923.00 to $149,333.00 / Per Year
OPEN PERIOD:	Tuesday, April 01, 2014 to Tuesday, September 30, 2014
SERIES & GRADE:	GS-2210-09/15
POSITION INFORMATION:	Full Time - Multiple Appointment Types
PROMOTION POTENTIAL:	15
DUTY LOCATIONS:	Few vacancies in the following location(s):

Gunter AFB, AL   View Map
Maxwell AFB, AL   View Map
Edwards AFB, CA   View Map
El Segundo, CA   View Map
Palmdale, CA   View Map
More Locations (36)

This position starts at GS-9 and can progress to GS-15. You can get hired into this position anywhere from GS-9 to GS-14.

36 locations for this job!

Veterans Preference applies to this posting.

WHO MAY APPLY:	United States Citizens
SECURITY CLEARANCE:	Secret
SUPERVISORY STATUS:	No

JOB SUMMARY:
The mission of the United States Air Force is to *fly, fight* and *win*...in air, space and cyberspace.

To achieve that mission, the Air Force has a vision of Global Vigilance, Reach and Power. That vision orbits around three core competencies: Developing Airmen, Technology-to-Warfighting and Integrating Operations. Core competencies and distinctive capabilities are based on a shared commitment to three core values -- *integrity first, service before self, and excellence in all we do.*

These positions are being filled under **Expedited Hiring Authority (EHA) for Defense Acquisition Workforce Positions and Health Care Occupations**. The Secretary of the Air Force has delegated authority by the Office Of the Secretary of Defense to directly appoint individuals to select defense acquisition workforce positions, or "EHA Acquisition", pursuant to the Defense Acquisition Workforce Improvement Act (DAWIA) and 2) certain health care occupations, or "EHA Medical". Positions are located Air Force-Wide. Positions may be filled as permanent, temporary or term with a full-time or part-time work schedule. Pay will vary by geographic location. **Please read this Public Notice in its entirety prior to submitting your application for consideration.'"**

This Public Notice may be used to fill positions in other equivalent pay systems.

JOB SUMMARY:

The mission of the United States Air Force is to fly, fight and win...in air, space and cyberspace.

To achieve that mission, the Air Force has a vision of Global Vigilance, Reach and Power. That vision orbits around three core competencies: Developing Airmen, Technology-to-Warfighting and Integrating Operations. Core competencies and distinctive capabilities are based on a shared commitment to three core values -- integrity first, service before self, and excellence in all we do.

These positions are being filled under **Expedited Hiring Authority (EHA) for Defense Acquisition Workforce Positions and Health Care Occupations.** The Secretary of the Air Force has delegated authority by the Office Of the Secretary of Defense to directly appoint individuals to select defense acquisition workforce positions, or "EHA Acquisition", pursuant to the Defense Acquisition Workforce Improvement Act (DAWIA) and 2) certain health care occupations, or "EHA Medical".

> This is a Direct Hire position and the AF will be hiring throughout the year for these positions. They can hire as permanent, temporary or term with full-time or part-time work schedules.

Positions are located Air Force-Wide. Positions may be filled as permanent, temporary or term with a full-time or part-time work schedule. Pay will vary by geographic location. **Please read this Public Notice in its entirety prior to submitting your application for consideration.'"**

This Public Notice may be used to fill positions in other equivalent pay systems.

DUTIES:

> Keywords in **BOLD**

- Work involves ensuring the **confidentiality, integrity, and availability of systems, networks**, and data through the planning, analysis, development, implementation, maintenance, and enhancement of **information systems security programs, policies, procedures, and tools**.

- Utilizes knowledge of **information technology principles, methods**, and security regulations and policies to administer various information security programs.

- Promotes awareness of **security issues among management** and ensures **sound security principles** are implemented to ensure protection of information transmitted to the organization, among organizations, and from the organization to the **local or wide area networks, the World Wide Web, or other communication nodes**.

- **Conducts risk assessments** to identify possible security violations. **Controls and protects all cryptographic material** and administers applicable access programs.

QUALIFICATIONS REQUIRED:

SPECIALIZED EXPERIENCE: For GS-9: 1 year of specialized experience equivalent to the GS-07 that was demonstrated knowledge of computer requirements and techniques in carrying out project assignments consisting of several related tasks, such as typically is the case in **development of minor modifications to parts of a system on the basis of detailed specifications provided**. The assignments must have shown completion of the following, or the equivalent: **Analysis of the interrelationships of pertinent components of the system; Planning the sequence of actions necessary to accomplish the assignment; and Personal responsibility for at least a segment of the overall project.**

> Make sure your resume shows the One Year Specialized Experience clearly for the grade level you are targeting.

For GS-11: 1 year of specialized experience equivalent to the GS-09 that demonstrated accomplishment of computer project assignments that required a range of knowledge of computer requirements and techniques demonstrated accomplishment of computer project assignments that required a range of knowledge of computer requirements and techniques. For example, assignments would show, on the basis of general design criteria provided, experience in developing modifications to parts of a system that required significant revisions in the logic or techniques used in the original development. Accomplishments, in addition to those noted for the GS-9 level, normally involve the following, or the equivalent: Knowledge of the customary approaches, techniques, and requirements appropriate to an assigned computer applications area or computer specialty area in an organization; Planning the sequence of actions necessary to accomplish the assignment where this entailed coordination with others outside the organizational unit and development of project controls; and Adaptation of guidelines or precedents to the needs of the assignment. ....

KNOWLEDGE, SKILLS AND ABILITIES (KSAs):

Your qualifications will be evaluated on the basis of your level of knowledge, skills, abilities and/or competencies in the following areas:

> Be sure to cover KSAs in your resume. The best way is to give examples.

1. **Knowledge of Information Technology security principles**, concepts, practices, systems software, database software, and immediate access storage technology to carry out activities leading to security certification or accreditation.

2. Ability to **assess risk factors** and **advise on vulnerability to attack** from a variety of sources and procedures and methods for protection of systems and applications.

3. **Knowledge of Local Area Network security requirements** and techniques for protecting computer systems from viruses, data tampering, and unauthorized system entry.

4. **Knowledge of commonly applied telecommunications principles, concepts, and methodologies**, operating characteristics and capabilities of systems, media, equipment, and related software systems, processes and procedures.

STEP 3

PART-TIME OR UNPAID EXPERIENCE: Credit will be given for appropriate unpaid and or part-time work. You must clearly identify the duties and responsibilities in each position held and the total number of hours per week.

ARE YOU USING YOUR EDUCATION TO QUALIFY? You MUST provide transcripts to support your educational claims. Education must be accredited by an accrediting institution recognized by the U.S. Department of Education.

FOREIGN EDUCATION: Education completed in foreign colleges or universities may be used to meet the requirements. You must show proof the education credentials have been deemed to be at least equivalent to that gained in conventional U.S. education program. It is your responsibility to provide such evidence when applying.

HOW YOU WILL BE EVALUATED:

Your latest resume will be used to determine your qualifications.

Your application package (resume, supporting documents, and responses to the questionnaire) will be used to determine your eligibility, qualifications, and quality ranking for this position. Please follow all instructions carefully. Errors or omissions may affect your rating or consideration for employment.

> Important: Your Questionnaire answers will be compared to your resume. Make sure your resume demonstrates your skill level.

Your responses to the questionnaire may be compared to the documents you submit. The documents you submit must support your responses to the online questionnaire. If your application contradicts or does not support your questionnaire responses, you will receive a rating of "not qualified" or "insufficient information" and you will not receive further consideration for this job.

Applicants who disqualify themselves will not be evaluated further.

To apply for this position, you must provide a complete Application Package which includes:

1. Your Resume (your latest resume will be used to determine your qualifications)

If you submit more than one copy of your resume, only the most recent (latest) version will be reviewed. The latest timestamp will be used to determine which version of your resume is "most recent". It is your responsibility to check the status and timestamp of all documents you submit as part of your application.

> Be sure to add your hours per week and month and year of employment.

For qualification determinations your resume must contain hours worked per week and dates of employment (i.e., hours per week and month/year to month/year or month/year to present). If your resume does not contain this information, your application may be marked as insufficient and you will not receive consideration for this position.

2. A complete Occupational Questionnaire

3. Additional Required Documents (see Required Documents section below). Ensure all submitted documents contain your full name, address, phone number and last four digits of your social security number.

> Do not include your whole SSN on any documents.

HOW TO APPLY:

The complete Application Package must be submitted by 11:59 PM (EST) on Tuesday, September 30, 2014

To begin the process, click the Apply Online button to create an account or log in to your existing USAJOBS account. Follow the prompts to complete the occupational questionnaire. Please ensure you click the Submit My Answers button at the end of the process.
To fax supporting documents you are unable to upload, click here for the required cover page. This Vacancy ID is 1079939. Fax your documents to 1-478-757-3144.

If you cannot apply online:
1. Click the following link to view and print the questionnaire View Occupational Questionnaire
2. OPM Form 1203-FX must be provided to show your responses to the occupational questionnaire. The numbering sequence on the OPM Form 1203-FX will not match the Occupational Questionnaire. Section 25 of the Occupational Questionnaire restarts with number one, so when entering your responses please continue regardless of number sequence. This issue has been identified and will be resolved as soon as possible.

PLEASE NOTE: It is the applicant's responsibility to verify that information entered, uploaded, or faxed (i.e., resume) is received, accurate and submitted by the closing date. You may verify your documents have been processed with your application package successfully by clicking here. Uploaded documents may take up to one hour to clear the virus scan. Faxed documents take 2-3 business days to process.

Human Resources WILL NOT modify or change any answers submitted by an applicant.

REQUIRED DOCUMENTS:

The following documents are required and must be provided with your application for this Public Notice:
Online Application (Questionnaire)
1) Resume (must include beginning/ending month & year for each employment period)
2) Transcripts (must contain the university logo, can be a copy)
3) Registration/License, active, current registration if applicable for the position

> The best format for the federal resume is the reverse chronological resume that begins with your Work Experience and dates of each employer or assigned base.

4) Veterans' Preference - a copy of your DD Form 214 which must include character of service or a Statement of Service/Proof of Service which must include service dates and character of service. In addition, if claiming 10 point preference you must submit a VA Letter or a disability determination from a branch of the Armed Forces (or documentation of purple heart, if applicable) and a SF 15 (Application for 10-point veteran preference).

IF APPLICABLE: A military service member's statement of service/certification will be accepted IF a terminal leave form or DD214 cannot be provided. The statement/certification should indicate member's separation from active duty is within 120 days of the closing date of this announcement. It must

> They will accept the Statement of Service if you do not have your DD 214 yet.

be signed by, or by direction of, the adjutant, personnel officer, or commander of your unit or higher headquarters and must indicate when your terminal leave will begin, your rank, dates of active duty service, the type of discharge and character of service (i.e. honorable). Your preference and/or appointment eligibility will be verified prior to appointment. Military members may be appointed before the effective date of their military retirement/separation if member is on terminal leave.

STEP 3

Army Installation Management Agency

Job Title: Hotel Customer Services Relations Assistant
Department: Department of the Army
Agency: Army Installation Management Command
Hiring Organization: Dragon Hill Lodge, IMCOM G-9, Armed Forces Recreation Center
Job Announcement Number: FEFX-14-09 1080462 SEC

SALARY RANGE:	$7.25 to $14.14 / Per Hour
OPEN PERIOD:	Monday, March 24, 2014 to Wednesday, April 16, 2014
SERIES & GRADE:	NF-1101-01
POSITION INFORMATION:	Part Time 20 hours - Permanent
PROMOTION POTENTIAL:	01
DUTY LOCATIONS:	1 vacancy in the following location: South Korea View Map
WHO MAY APPLY:	United States Citizens
SECURITY CLEARANCE:	Not Applicable
SUPERVISORY STATUS:	No

> Keywords are in bold.

DUTIES:

Performs **customer service relations** work that contributes toward the well-being of guests and the protection and safety of other employees and government property. **Performs routine security checks** to insure buildings, gates and equipment are properly locked or secured. **Inspects grounds** for fire, break-in, vandalism or trespassing. As required, checks identification of persons. **Uses tact and diplomacy** to deny entrance to unauthorized personnel. Ensures that patrons comply with applicable rules and standards. Must at times be **persuasive and forceful in dealing with persons whose conduct is unacceptable**. Reports incidents to proper authority. Maintains log of incidents and reports.

Ensures compliance with fire, safety, and security standards. Ensures all force protection technical systems such as fire alarms, intrusion detection systems, and CCTV, where applicable, are operating and maintained. In support of 24-hour hotel operations and limited third shift staffing, maintains an up-to-date working knowledge of all departmental functions necessary to ensure contingency of operations and guest services during the evening and night hours. Maintains a working knowledge of all **computer and emergency systems**. Works in conjunction and in **full cooperation with the military police, fire department, and other emergency response officials**. Operates a motor vehicle and performs other duties as assigned.

QUALIFICATIONS REQUIRED:

> These are the minimum qualifications that you have to prove in your resume.

Related experience as described above. Must possess **excellent customer services relations skills** in order to **communicate tactfully** in attending to the needs of guests and enforce the various **policies, requirements and rules of the facility** for which employed. Must be able to operate and use the various safety and other electronic and automated equipment involved in providing to the **well-being of guests** and the **protection and safety of employees and government property**. A **valid driver's license** is required

The USAJOBS vacancy announcement will have a link to view the Assessment Questionnaire (part 2 of your application) in Application Manager:

HOW TO APPLY: Back to top

To apply for this position, you must provide a complete Application Package which includes:
- Completed Resume – (Required) For more information click on "How To Prepare A Resume"
- Completed Questionnaire – (Required)
- Other supporting documentation as required. Please see the required documents section to determine if there are other documents you are required to submit.

To preview the questionnaire, please go to View Assessment Questions

---

Sample Assessment Questionnaire in Application Manager:

LEVEL DESCRIPTIONS

A- I have not had education, training or experience in performing this task.
B- I have had education or training in performing the task, but have not yet performed it on the job.
C- I have performed this task on the job. My work on this task was monitored closely by a supervisor or senior employee to ensure compliance with proper procedures.
D- I have performed this task as a regular part of a job. I have performed it independently and normally without review by a supervisor or senior employee.
E- I am considered an expert in performing this task. I have supervised performance of this task or I am normally the person who is consulted by other workers to assist them in doing this task because of my expertise.

3. Uses the FAR and DFAR to evaluate sources, negotiate prices and award procurements.

4. Makes purchases involving commercial requirements.

5. Makes non-competitive open market purchases.

6. Makes competitive open market purchases for repeat vendors.

7. Evaluate sources, negotiate and award procurements.

8. Awards purchase orders for supplies.

9. Reviews purchase order provisions to determine regulatory compliance or to improve competition.

10. Maintains purchase order logs, purchase order files and reference materials.

11. Utilizes a Federal contracting/procurement system to process solicitations, awards and/or modifications.

12. Performs market research, identifies potential vendors and creates the solicitation package.

13. Evaluates offers, conduct price analysis for reasonableness and recommends award to the Contracting Officer.

14. Identifies the circumstances prohibiting contract modification.

15. Prepares contract modification using proper procedures and in accordance with existing regulations.

16. Researches applicable contact clauses and provisions for purchases that involve special handling then determine the best method of delivery.

17. Reviews past performance, identifies potential vendors and creates solicitation packages.

18. Perform pre-solicitation review and planning, including review of previous history and the procurement package to ensure completeness and readiness for procurement action.

19. Performs market research to determine availability of the product or producers.

20. Perform evaluation of quotes or offers received.

21. Prepares Contractor Performance History Requests; interprets responses to determine any need for pre-award survey, and prepares Purchase Order or Contract Award documentation.

22. Identifies Purchase Requests for any of the following requirements: small business determination, first article test, government furnished property, or pre-award surveys.

23. Performs evaluation of offers, comparative price analysis for reasonableness and recommends award.

24. Analyzes, develops, and solicits requests for quotations (RFQ) from local and non-local commercial vendors.

> Give yourself all the credit that you can when selecting your multiple choice answers.
>
> Cover the knowledge, skills, and abilities in your federal resume.

STEP 4

Analyze Your Core Competencies

Besides specialized experience, education, and technical skills, what "value-added" competencies can you offer a supervisor?

What are competencies?

OPM defines a competency as a measurable pattern of knowledge, skills, abilities, behaviors, and other characteristics that an individual needs to perform work roles or occupational functions successfully. Successful job performance requires a broad range of competencies, such as technical knowledge, analytical abilities, and interpersonal skills. "Competencies can be seen as <u>basic qualities that employees should exhibit in the work place to maximize their potential for the government</u>."

Examples

- Are you a team leader who listens to team members' ideas, resolves problems quickly, strives to meet timelines, creates effective plans for training and execution, and gains cooperation and consensus during a project?

- Are you an IT specialist who, in addition to performing all the technical elements of the job, talks to customers about their IT problems, requests, and needs? Are you creative in coming up with solutions to problems?

- Are you an administrative professional who is customer-focused, follows up on inquiries, responds efficiently and effectively, and cares about the dilemmas that customers face?

Which Agencies Use Core Competencies?

The Veterans Administration, Office of Personnel Management, U.S. Marine Corps, Defense Finance & Accounting Service, and many other federal agencies are looking for qualified and skilled applicants who are also skilled in certain core competencies.

How Do I Use Core Competencies When Applying for Jobs?

These characteristics go above and beyond skills. You can stand out in a government resume, question/essay narrative, or behavior-based interview by highlighting these competencies. Study this step and determine the top five or ten competencies that make you a stand-out employee in your field of work. Add these competencies to your resume in the work experience descriptions for a stronger federal resume!

Veterans Administration Competencies

Find your core competencies and check them off the list. Add a few of these competencies into the "duties" section of your work experience.

Interpersonal Effectiveness

- ❑ Builds and sustains positive relationships.
- ❑ Handles conflicts and negotiations effectively.
- ❑ Builds and sustains trust and respect.
- ❑ Collaborates and works well with others.
- ❑ Shows sensitivity and compassion for others.
- ❑ Encourages shared decision-making.
- ❑ Recognizes and uses ideas of others.
- ❑ Communicates clearly, both orally and in writing.
- ❑ Listens actively to others.
- ❑ Honors commitments and promises.

Customer Service

- ❑ Understands that customer service is essential to achieving our mission.
- ❑ Understands and meets the needs of internal customers.
- ❑ Manages customer complaints and concerns effectively and promptly.
- ❑ Designs work processes and systems that are responsive to customers.
- ❑ Ensures that daily work and the strategic direction are customer-centered.
- ❑ Uses customer feedback data in planning and providing products and services.
- ❑ Encourages and empowers subordinates to meet or exceed customer needs and expectations.
- ❑ Identifies and rewards behaviors that enhance customer satisfaction.

Flexibility/Adaptability

- ❑ Responds appropriately to new or changing situations.
- ❑ Handles multiple inputs and tasks simultaneously.
- ❑ Seeks and welcomes the ideas of others.
- ❑ Works well with all levels and types of people.
- ❑ Accommodates new situations and realities.
- ❑ Remains calm in high-pressure situations.
- ❑ Makes the most of limited resources.
- ❑ Demonstrates resilience in the face of setbacks.
- ❑ Understands change management.

STEP 4

Veterans Administration Competencies cont.

Creative Thinking
- ❑ Appreciates new ideas and approaches.
- ❑ Thinks and acts innovatively.
- ❑ Looks beyond current reality and the "status quo".
- ❑ Demonstrates willingness to take risks.
- ❑ Challenges assumptions.
- ❑ Solves problems creatively.
- ❑ Demonstrates resourcefulness.
- ❑ Fosters creative thinking in others.
- ❑ Allows and encourages employees to take risks.
- ❑ Identifies opportunities for new projects and acts on them.
- ❑ Rewards risk-taking and non-successes and values what was learned.

Systems Thinking
- ❑ Understands the complexities of the agency and how the "product" is delivered.
- ❑ Appreciates the consequences of specific actions on other parts of the system.
- ❑ Thinks in context.
- ❑ Knows how one's role relates to others in the organization.
- ❑ Demonstrates awareness of the purpose, process, procedures, and outcomes of one's work.
- ❑ Encourages and rewards collaboration.

Organizational Stewardship
- ❑ Demonstrates commitment to people.
- ❑ Empowers and trusts others.
- ❑ Develops leadership skills and opportunities throughout organization.
- ❑ Develops team-based improvement processes.
- ❑ Promotes future-oriented system change.
- ❑ Supports and encourages lifelong learning throughout the organization.
- ❑ Manages physical, fiscal, and human resources to increase the value of products and services.
- ❑ Builds links between individuals and groups in the organization.
- ❑ Integrates organization into the community.
- ❑ Accepts accountability for self, others, and the organization's development.
- ❑ Works to accomplish the organizational business plan.

Transportation Security Administration Core Competencies

The Transportation Security Administration (TSA) has posted its catalog of competencies containing both core and technical competencies at **www.tsa.gov/assets/pdf/competencies_and_definitions.pdf**. Below is a sampling of core competency definitions from the catalog.

Accountability	Holds self and others accountable for measurable high-quality, timely, and cost-effective results; determines objectives, sets priorities and delegates work; accepts responsibility for mistakes; complies with established control systems and rules.
Administration and Management	Applies business and management principles involved in strategic planning, resource allocation, and coordination of people and resources in support of organizational operations.
Administrative Procedures and Tasks	Performs administrative responsibilities following guidelines and procedures; provides guidance to others; coordinates services, researches problems, and recommends changes.
Arithmetic and Mathematical Reasoning	Performs computations such as addition, subtraction, multiplication, and division correctly; solves practical problems by choosing appropriately from a variety of mathematical techniques such as formulas and percentages.
Attention to Detail	Is thorough and precise when accomplishing a task with concern for all aspects of the job involved; double-checks the accuracy of information and work products to provide consistently accurate and high-quality work.
Coaching & Mentoring	Provides clear, behaviorally specific performance feedback; makes suggestions for improvement in a manner that builds confidence and preserves self-esteem; works with individuals to develop improvement plans and achieve performance goals.
Command Presence	Demonstrates confidence, credibility, and professionalism in presence, demeanor, and conduct in performance of duties within the work environment.
Conflict Management	Encourages creative tension and differences of opinions; anticipates and takes steps to prevent counter-productive confrontations; manages and resolves conflicts and disagreements in a constructive manner.
Conscientiousness	Demonstrates responsible and dependable behavior; takes responsibility for personal performance through a high level of effort and commitment.

Department of Homeland Security (DHS) Competencies

The DHS competencies are comparable with those for DoD, IC, and OPM including the following communication skills:

- Report writing
- Verbal/speech
- Problem solving / Decision-making

The other competencies for DHS are focused on overall requirements for the Department.

OPM Competencies

The OPM competencies related to the DoD requirements in the following areas:

- Interpersonal skills
- Teamwork, learning
- Decision making
- Customer service
- Accountability

DoD Competencies

As listed in the DoD Competencies and compared with the DHS, OPM, and IC the most important/ reoccurring requirements were the following:

- Interpersonal skills
- Integrity
- Written and oral communication
- Continual learning
- Strategic thinking
- Team building
- Accountability
- Decisiveness
- Customer service
- Problem solving
- Technical credibility
- Enterprise-wide perspective

From https://nstii.com/content/core-competencies

Office of Personnel Management, Senior Executive Service, Executive Core Qualifications

Leading Change	Leading People	Results Driven	Business Acumen	Building Coalitions
Definitions				
This core qualification involves the ability to bring about strategic change, both within and outside the organization, to meet organizational goals. Inherent to this ECQ is the ability to establish an organizational vision and to implement it in a continuously changing environment.	This core qualification involves the ability to lead people toward meeting the organization's vision, mission, and goals. Inherent to this ECQ is the ability to provide an inclusive workplace that fosters the development of others, facilitates cooperation and teamwork, and supports constructive resolution of conflicts.	This core qualification involves the ability to meet organizational goals and customer expectations. Inherent to this ECQ is the ability to make decisions that produce high-quality results by applying technical knowledge, analyzing problems, and calculating risks.	This core qualification involves the ability to manage human, financial, and information resources strategically.	This core qualification involves the ability to build coalitions internally and with other federal agencies, state and local governments, nonprofit and private sector organizations, foreign governments, or international organizations to achieve common goals.
Competencies				
Creativity and Innovation	Conflict Management	Accountability	Financial Management	Partnering
External Awareness	Leveraging Diversity	Customer Service	Human Capital Management	Political Savvy
Flexibility	Developing Others	Decisiveness	Technology Management	Influencing/ Negotiating
Resilience	Team Building	Entrepreneurship		
Strategic Thinking		Problem Solving		
Vision		Technical Credibility		

STEP 5

Analyze Vacancy Announcements for Keywords

Keywords and Phrases for Your Outline Format Federal Resume

You can find keywords for your federal resume from the vacancy announcements. Adding keywords is important for both a federal resume and a private industry resume. You can analyze the following sections: Duties, Specialized Experience, KSAs, and the Questionnaire. The ALL CAP WORDS in an Outline Format resume are phrases and keywords from the announcements. The human resources specialist and supervisor will recognize these skills from their announcement. Your goal is to match your resume as closely as possible to your target announcement and demonstrate that you DO have the experience for their position.

Where Do I Find Keywords?

- **Vacancy Announcements**: Focus your search in these sections: Duties, Specialized Experience, Qualifications, and the Assessment Questionnaire.

- **Agency or Organizational Mission:** You may find this in the vacancy announcement or on the agency's website.

- **Core Competencies**: See Step 4 for more information about core competencies.

- **Occupational Standards**: It's not widely known yet that occupational standards are superb sources for keywords to use in your resume!

How Do I Find Keywords?

Find ONE GOOD target vacancy announcement. Analyze the Duties, Qualifications, and Specialized Experience sections for keywords. Find words (nouns or verbs) that are repeated over and over again. These will be the keywords. Make a list of keywords and build your resume content using this first set of keywords.

Now MATCH the keywords and add them to your resume.

Once you have drafted a basic resume, you MUST MATCH this resume to these keywords. Don't try to use the same resume to apply for a number of vacancy announcements.

Steps to Finding Keywords in a Vacancy Announcement

1. Save the vacancy announcement as an html file.

2. You will be reviewing these sections from the announcement for keywords:
   - ✪ Duties
   - ✪ Qualifications
   - ✪ Specialized Experience
   - ✪ Questionnaires
   - ✪ Agency or organization mission

3. Copy and paste these sections from the announcement into a word processing program such as Word or WordPerfect.

4. Enlarge the type to 14 or 16 points to make the print more readable.

5. Separate each sentence by increasing the line spacing for the entire document.

6. Delete useless words such as "the incumbent will" or "duties will encompass a variety of tasks including".

7. Underline or highlight keywords and skills that are significant to the position, such as "identifying deficiencies in human performance" and "recommending changes for correction."

How Many Keywords Do I Need?

At a minimum, include at least five to seven keywords in your resume. However, the more keywords you can include to help translate your experience into terms that the human resources specialist can clearly identify, the greater your chances of having the HR specialist understand how your qualifications match the desired qualifications in the vacancy announcement.

In the examples on the following pages, the found keywords are identified in bold type as well as listed at the end of each example.

Keywords can be found in the Duties and Qualifications sections of a vacancy announcement.

1702 Child and Youth Program Assistant (Entry, Skill and Target Level)

DUTIES:

Serves as a Child and Youth Program Assistant (CYPA) in one or more CYS programs. Maintains control of and accounts for whereabouts and **safety** of children and youth. Assists in **providing and leading planned activities** for program participants.

Helps establish a program environment that promotes **positive child and youth interactions** with other children, youth and adults.

Helps prepare, **arrange, and maintain indoor and outdoor activity areas** and materials to accommodate daily schedule.

Uses prepared curriculum/program materials and assists with developing a list of needed supplies and equipment.

Interacts with children and youth using approved child guidance and youth development techniques. Interacts professionally with **staff members, parents, and the Command.**

Supervises children and youth during daily schedule of **indoor and outdoor activities,** on **field trips,** outings and special events.

KEYWORDS

- Safety of children and youth
- Lead planned activities
- Ensure positive child and youth activities
- Manage indoor and outdoor activity areas
- Utilize program curriculum
- Prepare reports of signs of illness or abuse

STEP 5

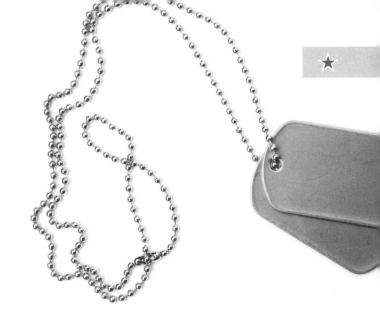

0189 Recreation Assistant, Dept. of the Army

MISSION:
The Kaiserslautern Arts & Cultural Center is full services Arts & Crafts facility offering **instructional programming** in various **technologically advanced computer-driven creative disciplines** like framing, quilting, sewing and many others.

DUTIES:
In a patron usage facility, circulates among patrons to assure service is satisfactory; receives and resolves **customer complaints;** provides **information and general instructions** on the use of **equipment, facilities and machinery.**

Assists patrons in use of the facility by **checking out equipment,** providing **safety instruction, demonstrating new equipment, teaching classes,** etc.

Plans, conducts, publicizes and arranges support for **special events, social activities, tournaments** and related functions. May provide **work guidance to other staff.**

KEYWORDS

- Recreation Assistant
- Instructor (Technology, Framing, quilting, sports, etc.)
- Customer services and complaint resolution
- Equipment demonstration and checkout
- Inventory control
- Safety instruction
- Special event coordinator

STEP 5

Keywords can be found in the OPM Classification Standards.

0341   Administrative Officer

CLASSIFICATION STANDARD

An administrative officer is a generalist. The total management process is his interest, and the proficiency required involves many aspects of management. **General management skills** are the paramount requirement. Though aspects such as **budget administration and personnel management** assume major importance in many positions and other aspects such as procurement and property management are also important in many jobs, no single functional, resource or service area forms a basis for the paramount skills.

Administrative officer positions typically include such duties and responsibilities as the following, or comparable duties:

1. Helping management to **identify its financial, personnel, and material needs and problems.**

2. **Developing budget estimates** and justifications; making sure that funds are used in accordance with the operating budget.

3. **Counseling management** in developing and maintaining sound organization structures, improving management methods and procedures, and seeing to the effective use of men, money, and materials.

4. **Collaborating** with personnel specialists in **finding solutions** to management problems arising out of changes in work which have an impact on jobs and employees.

5. **Advising on and negotiating contracts**, agreements, and cooperative arrangements with other government agencies, universities, or private organizations.

Administrative officer positions are mainly of two broad types. One type is the chief of a central administrative unit which provides services to a number of operating divisions, field offices, or other units each headed by an operating manager. The central administrative unit includes specialist positions in various areas such as **budget, data processing,** etc. The administrative unit chief has considerable authority to complete **personnel actions, obligate funds, make purchases,** etc.

KEYWORDS

- Management advisor
- Supervisor
- Budget advisor
- Problem-solving to management problems
- Advice on and negotiate contracts
- Data analyst

Keywords can be found in the KSAs and Quality Ranking Factors in Announcements.

0343 Management/ Program Analyst

DUTIES:

In this position, you will strengthen the Department's ability to perform homeland security functions by **developing policies,** conducting **special studies,** and providing **technical assistance.** Typical work assignments include:

- **Developing and evaluating policies** in assigned program areas such as reviewing **existing strategic and workforce management plans** and proposing potential changes to ensure plans represent organizational priorities and ensuring that comprehensive succession management planning is in place.
- **Analyzing existing management techniques**, processes, and plans for improving organizational effectiveness.
- **Evaluating policies and recommending actions** to achieve organizational objectives such as analyzing organizational programs and processes to determine whether current procedures efficiently accomplish objectives and provide sufficient controls necessary for sound management.

Quality Ranking Factor: Applicants who possess the following experience may be rated higher than applicants who do not possess this experience. The desired experience for this position includes work in **strategic planning, succession management, workforce planning and data analysis of human resource information.** Management desires experience in applying **data analysis, metrics and performance measure analysis** to **workforce planning and the development**, execution and improvement of organizational effectiveness planning.

KEYWORDS

- Conduct special studies
- Technical assistance on projects
- Develop policies for strategic planning and workforce planning
- Data analysis and performance measure analysis
- Workforce planning and development

Keywords can be found in the Specialized Experience section.

7401 Food and Beverage Attendant, Army Installation Management Agency

DUTIES:
Performs all of the following duties on a recurring basis;
Collects sales slips, total sales on **cash register,** accepts payment from patrons and makes change as necessary. Maintains related cash records. Keeps **work area clean and orderly.**

Sets up **food service counters** and steam tables with hot and cold foods and beverages. Prepares coffee and hot water for tea, fills beverage dispensers with juices and soft drinks.

Sets tables, seats guests, records guests' selections and turns in orders to the kitchen. Serves food, alcoholic and nonalcoholic beverages. Presents bill and receives payment. Cleans tables and immediate area.

Prepares fruits and vegetables for cooking and serving. Makes a variety of fruit and vegetable salads. Portions out food, cleans and prepares meats and seafood for cooking. Checks food during cooking to prevent overcooking. Unloads trucks and places contents in proper storage and use areas, brings supplies to work areas. Clean floors, walls and windows in kitchen, dining and storage areas.

Skill and Knowledge: **Able to work alone.** Know the proper use of special cleaning and sanitizing solutions. Know **simple food handling techniques. Able to work safely.** Able to serve uniform individual portions and avoid distractions when several guests ask for different items at the same time. Able to use simple arithmetic.

KEYWORDS

- Utilize cash register and collect payments
- Food handling
- Safety procedures
- Prepare fruits and vegetables for cooking and serving
- Seating tables, guests and customer services

Keywords can be found in the Questionnaires.

General Supply Specialist, GS-2001

For each task in the following group, choose the statement from the list below that best describes your experience and/or training. Darken the oval corresponding to that statement in Section 25 of the Qualifications and Availability Form C. Please select only one letter for each item.

A- I have not had education, training or experience in performing this task.

B- I have had education or training in performing the task, but have not yet performed it on the job.

C- I have performed this task on the job. My work on this task was monitored closely by a supervisor or senior employee to ensure compliance with proper procedures.

D- I have performed this task as a regular part of a job. I have performed it independently and normally without review by a supervisor or senior employee.

E- I am considered an expert in performing this task. I have supervised performance of this task or am normally the person who is consulted by other workers to assist them in doing this task because of my expertise.

4. **Interpret supply management regulations**, laws, concepts, principles to determine inventory management requirements.

5. **Use automated systems** to maintain records of supply items in inventory.

6. **Establish and implement policies**, procedural guidance and instruction for personal property control.

7. Recommend and **implement supply management policies** and procedures to **ensure operational accountability of property**.

KEYWORDS

- Interpret supply management regulations
- Utilize supply automated systems
- Implement personal property control policies
- Ensure operational accountability of property
- Provide customer services

And finally, keywords can be found in organizational mission statements!

This often-overlooked resource can yield some surprisingly useful keywords. Find the mission statement for the agency or organization online and see if you can locate a few more important keywords for your resume.

STEP 6

Write Your Outline Format and Paper Federal Resume

Many applicants consider this step to be the most difficult.

...which is why we want to introduce to you the Outline Format federal resume with keywords.

The Outline Format is highly regarded by human resources specialists for being very easy to read. The pertinent information that the HR specialist is looking for stands out much better in an Outline Format resume. Here are some of the key features:

- Small paragraphs are used for readability.
- ALL CAPS keywords match keywords in the announcement.
- Accomplishments are included in the resume.
- This format copies and pastes quickly and easily into USAJOBS.

Federal resumes are different from private industry resumes for a number of reasons. Here is a quick list of differences to keep in mind when you are converting your private industry resume into a federal resume.

Private Industry and TAP GPS Resume	Federal Resume
Typically 1-2 pages	3-5 pages based on specific character lengths (use full character lengths if possible)
Creative use of bold, underline, and other graphics	Text file, chronological, traditional format with no graphics; use CAPS for enhancement in lieu of graphics
No federal elements required (i.e., SSN, supervisor's name and phone, salary, veterans' preference, etc.)	Federal elements required (SSN, supervisor's name and phone, salary, veterans' preference, etc.)
Short accomplishment bullets focused on results	Accomplishment bullets focused on the details of "how" you attained results
Branded "headline"	Focus on the KSAs and competencies required in the announcement.
Keywords are important	Keywords are imperative
Focus on accomplishments; less details for position descriptions	Use blend of accomplishments and duties description with details
Profit motivated, product oriented, select customer base	Fiscal responsibility and grants, budgets, cost control, implementation of programs, legislation, serving the American public

Additional Special Considerations for Military

Military	Federal Resume
List dates of Reserve service and active duty service	Include approx. average hours for Reserve service, i.e., 20 years of Reserve service with deployments, equals six years of full-time work at 52 weeks per year
Include applicable awards and indicate justification for attaining award	List most awards and honors and include justification
Translate military acronyms and jargon	Translate most military acronyms and jargon, but use acronyms if the vacancy announcement uses the acronyms (i.e., DOD, DON, USMC, etc.)
Quantify and qualify military activities or acronyms	Quantify and qualify military activities or acronyms
Only include military schools/education related to the announcement	Include military service schools; indicate resident classes and total hours

Transitioning Military / Veterans

Contributed by Troy Johnson, Community Readiness Consultant / Transition Assistance Program Airman & Family Readiness Center, USAF

1. **Start your transition process no later than one year out** – Retirees can start their transition process two years out and those that are separating can start one year out. I would recommend that everyone start the transition process at least a year out; this will give them adequate time to properly prepare.

2. **Create your career catalog** – Gather all of your military documents and put them into a 3 ring binder, also called "I Love Me Books". Once this is done, you now can review your military career in its entirety.

3. **Develop your Master Resume** – Begin in a chronological order, starting with your current position. Don't worry about the length, and once you are done you should be to use this master resume and extract the information that is relevant to your career goals and objectives.

4. **Determine your career path** – Conduct career exploration and narrow down your primary and secondary career path, based on your values, interest and KSAs. Identify your industry first (Government, Contracting, or Corporate), then identify your targeted occupation / agency within that industry.

5. **Identify your barriers to employment** – You must identify your barriers (lack of experience, skills, education, personal, and credentials) by completing a Gap Analysis for each potential occupation of interest. Develop a plan of action to overcome them as soon as possible.

Wounded Warriors

Contributed by Dennis Eley, Jr, Wounded Warrior Coordinator, OCHR-San Diego Ops Center

1. **Determine your strongest skillset.** Visit the website www.mil2fedjobs.com and enter your military job title or MOS into the appropriate fields. This website cross walks your military job to equivalent civil service job titles that you may have experience in. Once you decide on a job title, this web-site links to USAJOBS and will conduct an immediate job search.

2. **What are you passionate about doing?** Passion is important in order to be happy with the work you will be doing. Granted, you will have to have the specialized experience to qualify for the job.

3. **If you have a severe disability, get a Schedule "A" letter.** If you are eligible for the letter, begin to look for transferrable skills to help build a strong resume for a new occupation.

4. **Plan to write the resume.** Tailor your resume to the job opportunity announcement to have a better chance at getting selected. Eliminate unrelated information from the resume.

5. **Translate any military jargon or language to civilian language** so the civilian HR professional can understand it. Even though you will be applying to federal jobs, the HR professional cannot assume that you have the required specialized experience. It must be in writing.

STEP 6

Military Spouses

Contributed by Employment Readiness Program Manager, Army Community Services, US

1. **Connect with the Army Community Service Employment Readiness Program Manager** prior to your arrival at your spouse's new duty station. Find out what spousal preference is/is not and how you may become eligible/ineligible. Find out the difference between Executive Orders 13473 and 12721 and how they may/may not apply to you.

2. **Put your resume, cover letter, and references on a thumb drive.** Understand the significance of a resume and how you will best fit into an organization. Understand what soft skills you possess.

3. **Practice who you are professionally** and understand that the organization/place may be culturally different than your own background. This is critical when moving to a new place as a military spouse. You may not have lived anywhere but in your hometown or your professional life was not entwined into the active duty environment. Understand that the sooner you acclimate to the military environment, the easier the transition will be for you.

4. **Research the organizations prior to the PCS move** and call the local civilian personnel office. Find out the expectation of the local civilian personnel office for a federal resume. This may vary from location to location. Prepare to have a 4-6 page resume providing details of how you achieved success on the job. Learn the mission statement for the organization that you are interested in. Talk to people who work in the organization.

5. **Attend as many seminars and workshops that are offered through Army Community Service as possible.** There are Certified Federal Job Search Trainers available to provide you with information and the opportunity to rehearse, practice, and participate in events that will allow you to enhance your professional skills. Understand that you are not the only spouse who is seeking employment.

US Navy Seabee Targeting Safety & Occupational Health Specialist

RICHARD CRANSTON

MOS: Utilitiesman – UT / E6
RECOMMENDED OCCUPATIONAL SERIES: Safety and Occupational Health Specialist (GS-0018)
RECOMMENDED TARGET GRADE LEVELS: GS - 9

REQUIRED ONE-YEAR SPECIALIZED EXPERIENCE:

EXPERIENCE: Your resume must demonstrate at least one year of specialized experience at or equivalent to the GS-09 grade level or pay band in the Federal service or equivalent experience in the private or public sector. Specialized experience is defined as experience that is typically in or related to the work of the position to be filled and has equipped you with the particular knowledge, skills, and abilities, to successfully perform the duties of the position. Specialized experience must demonstrate the following: 1) Coordinating workplace monitoring programs to support safety and occupational health initiatives; 2) Preparing safety and occupational reports outlining the origin, root cause, or contributing elements of mishaps and/or hazardous conditions; 3) Advising the organization on safety and occupational health awareness; and 4) Evaluating safety standards adopted by national safety associations, societies, or institutions to apply to organizational/ program processes.

BEFORE RESUME PROBLEMS:
- Too many words and keywords did not stand out
- The real "before" resume was 9 pages and it was in "landscape" format
- Too much information
- Training and certification lists were extremely long (originally total 4 pages)

AFTER RESUME SOLUTIONS:
- KEYWORDS AND KSAS are featured in Headline format in ALL CAPS
- Keywords are directly taken from the vacancy announcement
- Impressive accomplishments are featured clearly in the resume and descriptions were improved with more quantifiable numbers
- More emphasis on Knowledge of Regulations, Laws and Compliance
- Extra, repetitive language was taken out, so that the resume was totally focused on Safety and Occupational Health and past performance achievements
- Very detailed resume with specifics and proven accomplishments

HIRED! GS-0018-11 Safety and Occupational Health Specialist
Richard landed a permanent position: GS 7 target GS 11, USAG Yongsan.

"The program is a 3 year program. The first 2 years are for training. I start as GS-07 the first year, GS-09 the second year, and GS-11 my third year. Advancement is guaranteed as long as I keep up my end of the bargain and complete all my assigned tasks. My first task is 15 weeks of school in Alabama. I started at USAG Yongsan but after spending a few weeks with the engineering corps on a developmental assignment they wanted to hire me. Over the next 2 years I will receive OJT and other schools to receive civilian certifications important to the Safety Community. The Safety manager here called the Safety manager there and the next thing I know is relocate to the Corps to finish my internship."

RICHARD CRANSTON
88801 OKIE RD. * TAMPA, FL 32097 * Phone 9-888-888-8888
Cellular Phone 888-888-8888
E-Mail Richard.Cranston@ymail.com

SUMMARY OF EXPERIENCE

Coordinate and implement Occupational Safety and Health (OSH) Policies. Identify and interpret general industry 29CFR1910 and construction 29CFR1926 OSHA regulations and apply those standards to their work environment. Review plans and conduct risk analysis as well as trend analysis. Perform mishap investigations and maintain programs in hazard abatement, respiratory protection, fire safety, ergonomics, and hazardous materials management. Disseminate safety information and conduct employee training. Organize and manage monthly Safety Committee meetings and quarterly Safety Council meetings. Responsible for record keeping to include, employee medical surveillance, Industrial Hygiene Surveys, and work site inspections.

TECHNICAL SKILLS

Forklift Thru 12000LB -2007	Risk Management – 1998
Truck Dump 10CY – 2007	Risk Assessment – 1998
Truck Thru 15Tons- 2009	Site Inspections – 2001
Water Distribution Systems – 2005	Technical Writing – 2002
Electronic Distribution Systems – 2005	Employee Evaluation Writing - 2004
Disaster Preparedness Operations and	Communications -1997
Training Specialist -2011	Reverse Osmosis Water Purification Unit - 2005
Safety Inspector – 2009	
Safety Technician – 2002	Boiler Operator – 2004
Environmental Management – 2001	Secret Clearance- 2009

PROFESSIONAL WORK EXPERIENCE

United States Naval Support Activity Bahrain
Manama, N/A Bahrain
Emergency Management Specialist, 7/2011 – Present

Provide security and logistic support to NAVCENT and Fifth Fleet units in support of Operation Enduring Freedom and Operation New Dawn. Maintains and operates installation facilities for 89 tenant commands with a DoD population of over 5,000 personnel. Advises command on how to integrate into the normal command organization the functions necessary to prepare for, defend against, and recover from major accidents, natural and man-made disasters; assists in the coordination with local, civic authorities on disaster response operations; conducts training for nuclear, biological, and chemical (NBC) warfare defense to include hazard awareness, individual protection, decontamination, and mission restoration; performs organizational maintenance on NBC defense equipment; uses equipment complying with procedures required by Nuclear Regulatory Commission license.

*Trained 17 fire fighting personnel in firefighting techniques, search and rescue, and overhaul.
* Expert in Natural and man-made disaster preparedness.
* Developed and implemented a command morale program that promoted company values and increased employee morale.

US Navy Seabee Targeting Safety & Occupational Health Specialist

* Inventoried and tracked $328K of chemical, biological, and radiological protective and decontamination equipment.
* Trained 50 employees in natural and man-made disaster preparedness and response.

United Sates Navy Construction Battalion Maintenance Unit 202
Kings Bay, GA United States
Safety Manager, 1/2008 - 7/2011

Provide contingency Public Works operations at forward operating bases and executes construction projects for Naval Installations. Coordinated the implementation of the Navy Occupational Safety and Health (NAVOSH) Program, Traffic Safety Program, and Recreational, Athletics, and Home Safety Program. Performed administrative and record keeping functions in support of the command safety organization. Identified and corrected hazards, unsafe work practices, and health hazardous conditions. Conducted periodic workplace monitoring and evaluations. Prepared various safety and mishap reports, maintained hazard abatement program documentation, and performed mishap investigations. Arranged or conducted indoctrination and periodic Navy OSH and safety training. Disseminated Navy OSH and safety program information throughout the chain of command.

* Formulate, develop, and coordinate all safety and loss control functions of the organization.
* Design and direct a program to reduce accidents, occupational illnesses, and exposure to long-term health hazards through safety-training of all managers, planned inspections, skill training, first-aid care, emergency preparedness, proper job instruction, new employee indoctrination, physical protection, planned job observation, rules and practices, job analysis/procedures, disposal procedures, and protective equipment.
* Responsible for identifying causes of past accidents.
* Expertly managed a 100% wall to wall inventory the central tool room consisting of $538K worth of tools. Identified and corrected $68K of discrepancies and raised validity levels by 35%.
* Managed a safety program that included industrial and construction safety. Supporting 2 projects valued at $1.2M.
* Recognized during a Naval Operational Readiness Inspection as managing the "model Safety Program" and increasing Occupational Safety and Health readiness by 53%.
* Hand selected by the Commanding Officer amongst 350 candidates to be the Safety Manager for a 72 personnel detachment to Haiti in response to the 7.4 magnitude earthquake in Haiti.
* Enforced an effective Safety Program in Haiti under an extremely high op-tempo. The program required an on site assessment and swift planning that required experience and knowledge of OSHA and Naval regulations.
* Conducted reviews of near misses and implemented daily safety training to encourage a environment of safety.

United States Navy Mobile Construction Battalion 7
Projects Supervisor - Various Locations, 1/2004 - 1/2008

Provide contingency construction overseas to support allied forces as well as humanitarian construction for host nations. Provides military and technical training for construction personnel. Plan, direct, or coordinate, activities concerned with the construction and maintenance of structures, facilities, and systems. Participate in the conceptual development of a construction project and oversee its organization, scheduling, budgeting, and implementation. To includes managing in specialized construction fields, such as carpentry, electrical, and plumbing.

United States Navy Nuclear Power Training Unit

STEP 6

Goose Creek, SC United States
Safety Technician, 1/2001 - 1/2004

Provide training and qualification for Officer and Enlisted students in the practical principles of naval nuclear propulsion. Review, evaluate, and analyze work environments and design programs and procedures to control, eliminate, and prevent injury caused by chemical, physical, or ergonomic factors. Conduct inspections and enforce adherence to laws and regulations governing the health and safety of individuals.

EDUCATION & CERTIFICATIONS

A.A., Construction Technology
Coastline Community College, Fountain Valley, CA United States, 2009

A.A., Applied Marine Engineering
Coastline Community College, Fountain Valley, CA United States, 2009

B.S., Homeland Security and Disaster Preparedness
Thomas Edison State College, Trenton, NJ United States, Expected 2014

Hazardous Materials Awareness
Department of Defense, Manama, N/A Bahrain, 2011

29 CFR 1910. General Industry Safety Standards
Occupational Safety and Health Administration, Jacksonville, FL United States, 2009

Introduction to Navy Occupational Safety and Health Ashore
Naval Safety and Environmental Training Center, Kings Bay, GA United States, 2009

29 CFR 1926. Construction Safety Standards
Occupational Safety and Health Administration, Gulfport, MS United States, 2009

SPECIAL TRAINING

VPP-Contractor Safety- 2012
VPP-Safety and Health Program Evaluation – 2012
VPP- The Voluntary Protection Programs for Industrial Hygiene/Bioenvironmental and Occupational Health -2012
VPP-Mishap Investigations -2012
VPP-History and Trend Analysis -2012
Anthropometry in Ergonomic Design -2012
Office Ergonomics -2012
Work-related Musculoskeletal Disorders (WMSD) of the Back -2012
Work-related Musculoskeletal (WMSD) of the Upper Extremities -2012
Workstation Design and Illumination -2012

The
Resume Place

11-Point Federal Resume Checksheet^{SM}

Richard Cranston
Occupational Safety & Health Specialist, GS 9/11

LENGTH: Is the resume 3 to 5 pages in length? *Total length is okay. The description of the current position is too short.*

ACCOMPLISHMENTS: Are accomplishments included for the last position or the most relevant position? *Yes, accomplishments are here, but they are not detailed enough.*

FORMAT: Is the resume in the Outline Format? *Not in the Outline Format.*

TYPEFONT: Is it easy to see keywords, either in ALL CAPS or boldface? *Okay.*

KEYWORDS: Does the resume have keywords from a particular occupational series? *Keywords are not featured.*

ONE YEAR SPECIALIZED EXPERIENCE: Is this clearly included in the resume? *Maybe.*

10 YEARS EXPERIENCE: Does the resume focus on the last 10 years? *Yes.*

RECENT AND RELEVANT: Does the resume feature recent and relevant for the target occupational series / job?
Yes. The last job is the relevant position and the only position.

MONTH, YEAR AND HOURS PER WEEK: Are these included for the last 10 years? *Yes.*

SALARY: Is salary information in the resume for positions in the last 10 years? *No.*

TARGETING TOWARD AN OCCUPATIONAL SERIES: Is the resume targeted toward an occupational series with the correct keywords? *Not at all.*

A sample blank 11-Point Federal Resume Checksheet is available on page 121.

STEP 6

The new federal resume was written in the Outline Format with keywords and accomplishments. This federal resume is in the "paper format" designed to UPLOAD into USAJOBS.

RICHARD CRANSTON
88801 OKIE RD. * TAMPA, FL 32097 * Phone 9-888-888-8888
Cellular Phone 888-888-8888
E-Mail Richard.Cranston@ymail.com

PROFESSIONAL PROFILE

- **Expert leader** skilled in all aspects of comprehensive safety and occupational health. Well-rounded grasp of safety issues' relation to human behavior and motivation, supervising to zero defects, no injuries and increased employee morale.
- **Knowledgeable** of relevant safety and occupational health policies and procedures, whether in the United States, at sea or in foreign countries. Extensively trained in OSHA and NAVOSH requirements.
- **Sought-after expert** advising management and organizations in safety and health matters, and a go-to authority who has answers and solves problems. Assists and advises Department Managers in all aspects of safety and occupational health.
- **Recognized for excellence** in managing "the model Safety Program", and hand-selected by Commanding Officer to be Safety Manager for special detachment to post-earthquake Haiti, responsible for 72 personnel under hazardous conditions and with fewer resources than normal.
- **Outstanding Manager** demonstrating responsibility with the equipment, finances and personnel entrusted to his authority. Delivers on-time or sooner, under-budget and with excellent safety records and certified inspections.

WORK EXPERIENCE

Naval Support Activity, Bahrain
Manama, 13 Bahrain

06/2011 – Present
Salary 98,000 per year, 60 hours per week
Supervisor: George Polo (9999999)
Permission to contact this Supervisor: Yes

EMERGENCY MANAGEMENT SPECIALIST

Provide security and logistic support to NAVCENT and Fifth Fleet units in support of Operation Enduring Freedom and Operation New Dawn. Maintain and operate installation facilities for 89 tenant commands with a DoD population of over 5,000 personnel.

PROVIDE ADVICE AND GUIDANCE TO MANAGERS AND ORGANIZATION ON SAFETY AND OCCUPATIONAL HEALTH AWARENESS MATTERS: Advise command on how to integrate into the normal command organization the functions necessary to prepare for, defend against, and recover from major accidents, natural and man-made disasters.

TRAIN EMPLOYEES AND MANAGERS IN SAFETY AND OCCUPATIONAL HEALTH SUBJECTS: Using knowledge of safety and occupational health policies and procedures, ensure maximum effectiveness in protecting personnel and work areas from unsafe practices and environments. Trained employees in natural and man-made disaster preparedness and response. Trained auxiliary firefighting personnel in firefighting techniques and search and rescue. Trained 50 employees in natural and man-made disaster preparedness and response.

KEY ACCOMPLISHMENTS:

- Developed and implemented a command morale program that promoted company values and increased employee morale.

- Inventoried and tracked $328K in chemical, biological and radiological protective and decontamination equipment to protect combat readiness.

- Trained 17 auxiliary firefighting personnel in firefighting techniques, search and rescue and overhaul, which increased the base's ability to control a fire, since the base does not have a fully manned fire department.

- Active member of the Integrated Training Team, which coordinates mass casualty drills throughout Europe and the Middle East, increasing the Navy's overall ability to function in the event coordinated attacks occur to multiple commands simultaneously.

- Recognized expert in natural and man-made disaster preparedness, trained in plotting the path of chemical clouds and determining half lives of a radiological attack. This capability allows the base to function overseas in a potentially hazardous environment.

Construction Battalion Maintenance Unit 202
Kings Bay, GA   United States

01/2008 – 06/2011
Salary 60,000 per year, 50 hours per week
Supervisor: Clint Pierre (retired) (888-888-8888)
Permission to contact this Supervisor: Yes

SAFETY MANAGER

Provided contingency Public Works operations at forward operating bases and executed construction projects for Naval Installations.

EVALUATE SAFETY STANDARDS TO APPLY TO PROGRAMS AND PROCESSES, ENSURE COMPLIANCE W/ REGULATORY GUIDELINES: Coordinated the implementation of the Navy Occupational Safety and Health (NAVOSH) Program, Traffic Safety Program, and Recreational, Athletics, and Home Safety Program. Arranged or conducted indoctrination and periodic Navy OSH and safety training. Disseminated Navy OSH and safety program information throughout the chain of command.

DEMONSTRATE KNOWLEDGE OF SAFETY AND OCCUPATIONAL HEALTH POLICIES, PROCEDURES: Performed administrative and record keeping functions in support of the command safety organization. Identified and corrected hazards, unsafe work practices, and health hazardous conditions.

RECOMMEND SPECIFIC TECHNIQUES AND PROCEDURES TO REDUCE UNSAFE ACTS OR CONDITIONS: Conducted periodic workplace monitoring and evaluations. Communicated recommendations in writing. Formulated, developed, and coordinated all safety and loss control functions of the organization using ESAMS database, Excel, and Word. Constantly communicated to higher authority command status and situational reports.

INVESTIGATE MISHAPS AND IMPLEMENT CORRECTIONS TO AVOID RECURRENCE: Responsible for investigating and identifying causes of incidents and managing the hazard abatement program. Prepared various safety and mishap reports, maintained hazard abatement program documentation, and performed mishap investigations.

PLAN AND IMPLEMENT SAFETY COURSES: Designed and directed programs to reduce accidents, occupational illnesses, and exposure to long-term health hazards through safety-training of all managers, planned inspections, skill training, first-aid care, emergency preparedness, proper job instruction, new employee indoctrination, physical protection, planned job observation, rules and practices, job analysis/procedures, disposal procedures, and ergonomics.

KEY ACCOMPLISHMENTS:

- Hand selected by the Commanding Officer from among 350 candidates to be the Safety Manager for a 72 personnel detachment to Haiti, in response to their 7.4 magnitude earthquake. Selection carried with it all the responsibilities normally carried out while in the United States but with less resource availability and very hazardous conditions. The end result of Haiti effort was zero reportable injuries and no lost time.

- Expertly managed a 100% wall-to-wall inventory of the central tool room consisting of $538K worth of tools. Identified and corrected $68K of discrepancies and raised validity levels by 35%.

- Managed a safety program that included industrial and construction safety as well as day-to-day shop safety. Supported 2 projects valued at $1.2M. Programs and industrial processes included welding, plumbing, steel work, carpenter shop, transportation bays, vehicle maintenance, hazardous materials management, ergonomics, respiratory protection, PPE, hearing conservation, asbestos program, PCBs, and mishap investigations.

- Recognized during a Naval Operational Readiness Inspection as managing the "model Safety Program" and increasing Occupational Safety and Health readiness by 53%.

Naval Mobile Construction Battalion 7
Gulfport, MS   United States

05/2004 – 01/2008
Salary 50,000 per year, 72 hours per week
Supervisor: Mr. Skyler (retired) (999-999-9999)
Permission to contact this Supervisor: Yes

PROJECTS SUPERVISOR

Provided contingency construction overseas to support allied forces as well as humanitarian construction for host nations in various locations worldwide. Provided military and technical training for construction personnel.

PROBLEM SOLVING: Participated in the conceptual development of a construction project and oversaw its organization, scheduling, budgeting, and implementation, including managing specialized construction fields, such as carpentry, electrical and plumbing. Planned, directed or coordinated activities concerned with the construction and maintenance of structures, facilities, and systems.

MANAGE COMPLEX PROJECTS: Maintained, updated, and distributed production schedules. Planned and assigned work, trained employees, authorized termination, discipline, and performance decisions of initially assigned crews. Supervised seven personnel during Hurricane Katrina Disaster Recovery efforts. Removed 65 tons of debris, placed 32,000SF of tarp, and cleared 50 miles of roadway. Supervised a mission essential construction assessment for a firebase in Afghanistan. Created bill of materials, scopes of work, and planning guidelines for future expansion.

ENSURE COMPLIANCE WITH REGULATIONS: Responsible for maintaining product quality standards by reading blueprints, building codes, mechanical codes, manufacture specifications, and adhering to safety procedures. Coordinated with Engineers and civilian contractors.

KEY ACCOMPLISHMENTS:

- During the entire Katrina effort no injuries were noted, due to proper planning, attention to detail, enforcement of PPE and standard operating procedures, and onsite inspections.

- Planned and estimated a 3,840 man hour project valued at just over $250,000. The plan included Safety, Environmental, and Quality Control Plans for each phase of the process. The project was completed one month ahead of schedule and no personnel were injured despite inclement weather, lack of resources, and a remote location.

- Supervised 13 personnel during military exercises in Mississippi in the hottest part of the year. Due to proper personnel management and practice of proper safety procedures no personnel received any type of heat injury.

- Managed all camp facilities for Special Forces Camp Heselton, Afghanistan. Identified 137 maintenance discrepancies and initiated corrective measures and repairs. This greatly increased morale of Special Forces overseas.

Naval Nuclear Power Training Unit, Charleston
Goose Creek, SC   United States

01/2001 – 01/2004
Salary 45,000 per year, 40 hours per week
Supervisor: Mr. Buddy (912.573.3333)
USS Arleigh Burke DDG-51
Norfolk, VA   United States

02/1997 – 01/2001
Salary 40,000 per year, 72 hours per week
Supervisor: Mr. Sunny (retired) (912.573.3333)

EDUCATION

Coastline Community College Fountain Valley, CA United States
Associate's Degree 05/2009

Credits Earned: 60 Semester hours
Major: Marine Engineering **Minor:** Construction Technology

JOB RELATED TRAINING

Hazardous Materials Awareness Department of Defense 2011
29 CFR 1910. General Industry Safety Standards, Occupational Safety and Health Administration, 80hrs, 2009
Introduction to Navy Occupational Safety and Health Ashore Naval Safety and Environmental Training, 2009
29 CFR 1926. Construction Safety Standards, Occupational Safety and Health Administration, 80hrs, 2009
Mishap Investigations Ashore, Naval Safety and Environmental Training Center, 40hrs 2009
Journeyman Instructor Training Center for Personal and Professional Development 2009
Command Training Team Center for Personal and Professional Development 2009

ADDITIONAL INFORMATION
Coordinate and implement Occupational Safety and Health (OSH) Policies. Identify and interpret general industry 29CFR1910 and construction 29CFR1926 OSHA regulations and apply those standards to the work environment. Review plans and conduct risk analysis as well as trend analysis. Perform mishap investigations and maintain programs in hazard abatement, respiratory protection, fire safety, ergonomics, and hazardous materials management. Disseminate safety information and conduct employee training. Organize and manage monthly Safety Committee meetings and quarterly Safety Council meetings. Responsible for record keeping including, employee medical surveillance, Industrial Hygiene Surveys, and work site inspections.

Dawn McCallem

BEFORE GETTING HIRED: Volunteer Individual Deployment Support System Coordinator, Joint Base Anacostia-Bolling (JBAB)

RECOMMENDED OCCUPATIONAL SERIES: Human Resources
RECOMMENDED TARGET GRADE LEVELS: GS – II-I2

HUMAN RESOURCES SPECIALIST – ONE YEAR SPECIALIAZED EXPERIENCE KEYWORDS FOR THE FEDERAL RESUME:

- Human resources consultant
- Employee/labor relations analyst and problem-solver
- Expertise in human resources (hr) development and workforce shaping
- Knowledge of benefits programs
- Skill in classification, job analysis, and performance management
- Compensation programs expertise
- Skill in recruitment/staffing
- Knowledge of hr information systems
- Instruction, presentations, and briefings

HUMAN RESOURCES SPECIALIST – PPP-S

PPP Skills Options Codes include: EMC, STF, FSP, STP, and PHR.
Competencies include: Employee Relations, Staffing, Family Support Services, Strategic Planning, and Personnel.

HUMAN RESOURCES SPECIALIST – PRIVATE INDUSTRY RESUME KEYWORDS:

Compliance; Policy Development; Employee Relations; EEO/Affirmative Action; Workers Compensation; Training/Development; Recruitment & Retention; Benefits Administration; Labor Relations; Payroll Administration ; Strategic/Capabilities Planning; Employee Communications; Succession Planning; Organizational Design; Disaster Response

HIRED!

Good morning Ladies! I just wanted to share with you that I got a job as HR Director for a County in Texas. I had to interview with two judges and four commissioners - talk about intimidating! The judge later told me they had received I84 applications for the position, they interviewed nine candidates, & selected me! I am so very excited! This position was definitely worth the wait!! Thank you both so much for all you help - I am truly grateful! Have an outstanding weekend! -- Dawn McCallem

Above photo credit:
Dawn McCallem, Proud Member of American Military Spouses Choir, Successful Vocal Finalists for "America's Got Talent", Fall 2013. Published with permission by contestant.
AF spouse sings her way into America's hearts, By Shauna Jones, AFCEC Public Affairs, Published August 14, 2013; http://www.af.mil/News/ArticleDisplay/tabid/223/Article/466846/af-spouse-sin;
http://www.af.mil/News/Photos/tabid/129/igphoto/2000706019/Default.aspx

Dawn P McCallem
69 Michigan Ave., NW
Washington, DC 20032 US
Day Phone: 222-222-2222
Email: Dawn.McCallem.HR@gmail.com

Work Experience:

Novonics Corporation (govt contractor) Arlington, VA United States	**01/2010 - 01/2011** **Salary:** 91,000.00 USD Per Year **Hours per week:** 40

HUMAN RESOURCES MANAGER
Supervisor: Charles Polo (444-444-4444)
Okay to contact this Supervisor: Yes
Coordinated and maintained the company-wide human resources activities in the areas of compliance, recruiting, human resources policy development, Affirmative Action Plan, compensation and benefits administration for 130 employees across ten locations. Resolved very difficult employee relations issues in support of a wide variety of controversial conduct-related issues. Assessed and provided guidance on needs of employees, such as relocation, career resource development, time management, and goal setting. Utilized written and oral communication techniques sufficient to develop and deliver briefings, project papers, status/staff reports, and correspondence to managers to foster understanding and acceptance of findings and recommendations.
KEY ACCOMPLISHMENTS:
+Lowered health care renewal costs by $174,625.65 for the 2010/2011 plan year by moving from a fully insured plan to a partially self-funded plan.
+Prepared organization's Affirmative Action Plan, for the 2009/2010 plan year; communicated results and goals to management.
+Reduced sporadic and random hiring across the company by implementing a hiring process according to the Office of Federal Contract Compliance Programs (OFCCP) procedures
+Created, implemented, and trained managers on anti-bullying policy, reducing the number organization-wide bullying complaints.

J.R. Simplot Grand Forks, ND United States	**02/2008 - 08/2009** **Salary:** 75,000.00 USD Per Year **Hours per week:** 50

HUMAN RESOURCES MANAGER
Supervisor: David Buddy (777-777-7777)
Okay to contact this Supervisor: Yes
Managed seven-person human resources team providing support for 400 employees across recruitment, hiring, employee and labor relations, payroll and benefits, workers' compensation, and unemployment functions. Established strategic relationships with key organization individuals to assist in achieving the organization's strategic goals and objectives. Provided consultation and assistance to management team on complex and often controversial conduct-related issues. Established objectives, procedures and plans that met both long- and short-range goals. Participated in consensus building, negotiating, coalition building, and conflict resolution techniques to interact appropriately in highly charged emotional situations.
KEY ACCOMPLISHMENTS:
+Assisted in the implementation of organization's casualty/disaster response plan, which minimized the organization's exposure to liability in the event a loss or injury occurs.
+Participated in casualty and disaster response exercises carried out by the organization, which resulted in a quicker response time in emergency situations.
+Facilitated site succession planning; ensured seamless progress during periods of change.
+Improved employee retention by analyzing terminations and exit interviews for improvement opportunities and retention plan.
+Achieved 4% reduction in overtime costs through human resources effective tracking and analysis.

STEP 6

+Attained record-breaking seven-day completion time in negotiating labor contract.
+Implemented regular meetings incorporating union stewards to reduce the number of grievances filed and improve employer/labor relations. This resulted in a reduction of approximately one to two weekly grievances to one grievance every month or so.

Education:
Human Resources Certification Institute Alexandria, VA
Technical or Occupational Certificate 12/2006
Major: Professional Human Resources (PHR)

Troy State University Alamogordo (Holloman AFB), NM
Master's Degree 04/2004
GPA: 3.9 of a maximum 4.0
Major: Management **Minor:** Human Resources

University of Maryland University College Ramstein Germany
Bachelor's Degree 12/2002
GPA: 3.0 of a maximum 4.0
Major: Information Systems Management

Job Related Training: SPECIALIZED TRAINING:
+Boots to Business (SBA - 2012)
+Military Families in Transition (Zeiders/CNIC - 2012)

Additional Information:
ELIGIBLE: COMPETITIVE AND NONCOMPETITIVE SPOUSE SEEKING FEDERAL POSITION TRAINING INSTRUCTOR. Seeking a federal position utilizing my Noncompetitive Spouse Appointment of Certain Military Spouses and Competitive DoD Priority Placement Program.

COMPUTER SKILLS:
+Type 50+ WPM, PeopleSoft, JDE, SAP, DelTek, BalanceAAP, Microsoft Office

VOLUNTEER ACTIVITIES:
+Joint Base Anacostia and Bolling, Washington, DC, 4/2012 - present
INDIVIDUAL DEPLOYMENT SUPPORT SYSTEM VOLUNTEER: Provide assistance, support, and advocacy to service members and their families in preparation for deployments. Ensure families know that the Military and Family Support Center (MFSC) cares about them during their separation and MFSC is always available to them should they need assistance. Assess families' needs; provide information on referrals to appropriated resources; and follow procedures according to established standard operating procedures.
KEY ACCOMPLISHMENTS:
+As a command representative assistant, gathered approximately 150 command/unit contacts (on and off base) and compiled the information into an excel spreadsheet. Commands/units will be contacted to offer training of services: career/retention, deployment/readiness; life skills education.

+MEMBER OF THE US MILITARY WIVES CHOIR
+Performed at the Kennedy Center (May 2012)
+Recorded the song, "The Promise That We Make" (June 2012)

+NATIONAL COMMUNITY CHURCH VOLUNTEER
+Provide volunteer services for community activities.

Military Spouse Targeting Human Resources Position

The
Resume Place

11-Point Federal Resume Checksheet^{SM}

Dawn P McCallem
Target Human Resources Specialist, GS 11/12 positions

LENGTH: Is the resume 3 to 5 pages in length? *Length is okay.*

ACCOMPLISHMENTS: Are accomplishments included for the last position or the most relevant position?
Yes, accomplishments are here, not enough details about how the accomplishments were achieved

FORMAT: Is the resume in the Outline Format? *This is a USAJOBS federal resume, but not in the outline format with keywords.*

TYPEFONT: Is it easy to see keywords, either in ALL CAPS or boldface?
Type is okay, USAJOBS format.

KEYWORDS: Does the resume have keywords from a particular occupational series?
Keywords are not clearly presented for human resources specialist positions.

ONE YEAR SPECIALIZED EXPERIENCE: Is this clearly included in the resume? *Yes.*

10 YEARS EXPERIENCE: Does the resume focus on the last 10 years? *Yes.*

RECENT AND RELEVANT: Does the resume feature recent and relevant for the target occupational series / job?
Not sure which position will be most relevant for the target HR position.

MONTH, YEAR AND HOURS PER WEEK: Are these included for the last 10 years?
YES, you are in USAJOBS format.

SALARY: Is salary information in the resume for positions in the last 10 years?
YES. Good.

TARGETING TOWARD AN OCCUPATIONAL SERIES: Is the resume targeted toward an occupational series with the correct keywords?

It might be targeted toward Human Resources, but the specialized experience, KSAs and keywords are not featured.

A sample blank 11-Point Federal Resume Checksheet is available on page 121.

STEP 6

The new federal resume was written in the Outline Format with keywords and accomplishments. This is in the "paper format" designed to upload into USAJOBS. This resume is also written with Option Codes for the PPP-S Database.

Dawn P. McCallem
1727 Texas Road
San Antonio, TX 78258
Dawn.McCallem.HR@gmail.com
(888) 888-88888

SPOUSE PREFERENCE: Spouse of Active Duty USAF. Eligible for Consideration under Executive Order 13473, September 1, 2009 Non-competitive Appointment for Certain Military Spouses, and DoD Priority Placement Program.

CAREER OBJECTIVES: Human Resources Management Specialist GS-0201-11/12; Administration and Program Series, GS-0301-11; Program Analyst, GS-0343-11.

PPP Skills Options Codes include: EMC, STF, FSP, STP, and PHR. Competencies include: Employee Relations, Staffing, Family Support Services, Strategic Planning, and Personnel.

PROFESSIONAL PROFILE

- Human Resources (HR) professional with close to 10 years of broad and complex HR experience including benefits, compensation, STAFFING and recruiting, employee/labor relations, job analysis, performance management, human resources development and workforce shaping.
- Master's Degree in Management and Human Relations.
- Certification in Professional Human Relations.
- AWARD: Presidential Gold Medal - for serving more than 500 volunteer hours (June 2013)
- MEMBER OF THE US MILITARY WIVES CHOIR
- Runner-up in America's Got Talent, 2013; Performed at the Kennedy Center (May 2012); Recorded the song, "The Promise That We Make" (June 2012)
- Proven ability to plan and organize work independently, to identify problems and develop original and productive solutions, and to organize work independently.
- Accomplished trainer, skilled in working with diverse audiences.
- Flexible, highly competent, and professional team player with solid communication skills.

WORK EXPERIENCE:

INDIVIDUAL DEPLOYMENT SUPPORT SYSTEM VOLUNTEER Military & Family Life Support Center Joint Base Anacostia-Bolling Washington, DC Supervisor: Patricia Pierre (202-222-2222) Okay to contact this Supervisor: Yes	04/2012 – present Salary: $0 (volunteer) Hours per week: 8-16

ADVOCATE: Provide assistance, support, and advocacy to service members and their families in preparation for deployments.

SEPARATION COUNSELOR: Ensure families know that the Military and FAMILY SUPPORT Center (MFSC) cares about them during their separation and that MFSC is always available to them should they need assistance.

EXPERTISE providing counseling to employees concerning WORK AND FAMILY LIFE issues including information and referral to Employee Assistance Programs; providing services to military members, retirees, and family members. Assess clients' needs and concerns, such as relocation, career resource development and personal financial issues, and refer them to the appropriate advisor for assistance.

INTAKE ASSESSMENTS FOR FAMILY NEEDS: Assess family needs; provide information on referrals to appropriate resources; and follow procedures according to established standard operating procedures.

INSTRUCTOR: Contact Commands/units to offer training of services: career/retention, deployment readiness; and life skills education.

KEY ACCOMPLISHMENT:

- RESEARCHER / DATABASE UPDATES: As a command representative assistant, gathered approximately 150 command/unit contacts (on and off base) and compiled the information into an Excel spreadsheet.
- Participated in PLANNING AND COORDINATING the Military & Family Support Center Military Appreciation Expo and Hiring event attended by 70+ employers and 400+ job seekers.

HUMAN RESOURCES MANAGER	01/2010 - 01/2011
Novonics Corporation	Salary: $91,000.00/Year
Arlington, VA United States	Hours per week: 40
Supervisor: Charles Polo (444-444-4444)	
Okay to contact this Supervisor: Yes	

[Company is a government contractor providing management support to customers within the U.S. Department of Defense]

HUMAN RESOURCES CONSULTANT: Retained to spearhead special project to evaluate EMPLOYEE RELATIONS, Affirmative Action Plan and resolve controversial issues for 130 IT specialist contractors located in 9 US Cities and Japan for the US Navy Civilian Operations. Coordinated and maintained the full array of company-wide human resources activities in the areas including labor relations, recruiting, human resources policy development, job analysis and performance management, compensation, and benefits administration. Ascertained that all HR programs were compliant with applicable federal laws and regulations.

EMPLOYEE/LABOR RELATIONS ANALYST AND PROBLEM-SOLVER: Resolved very difficult EMPLOYEE RELATIONS issues in support of a wide variety of controversial conduct-related issues. Researched and evaluated laws, regulations, and precedent. Ensured that EMPLOYEE RELATIONS activities were compliant with applicable federal laws and regulations. Assessed and provided guidance on needs of employees, such as relocation, career resource development.

EXPERTISE IN HUMAN RESOURCES (HR) DEVELOPMENT and WORKFORCE SHAPING. Conducted needs assessments to identify and establish priorities regarding HR development activities. Experienced in processing personnel actions, such as interviewing, recruiting, selecting, and hiring candidates; promotions, transfers, layoffs, and terminations. Selected, implemented, and conducted employee training programs (e.g. leadership skills, harassment prevention). Provided coaching to management regarding effectively managing organizational talent.

KNOWLEDGE OF BENEFITS PROGRAMS. Responded to complex benefits questions. Managed outsourced benefits components. Conducted benefit program need assessments (e.g. benchmarking, employee surveys). Developed, implemented, administered, updated, and evaluated benefit programs. Communicated and trained workforce in benefit programs policies and processes. Administered organization's retirement and benefits program. Conducted fact-finding and research to administer the organization's injury compensation program; analyzed information related to on-the-job injuries and Worker's Compensation claims; provided training to supervisors and employees on practices and regulations relating to the injury compensation program.

SKILL IN CLASSIFICATION, JOB ANALYSIS, and PERFORMANCE MANAGEMENT. Advised managers and developing position descriptions. Determined the correct pay categories titles and levels of positions. Served on STRATEGIC management team addressing classification policy. Provided insight to establishing organizational structures that were efficient, cost-effective, and facilitated career development. Communicated distinctions in the position title levels with supporting criteria justification.

STEP 6

COMPENSATION PROGRAMS EXPERTISE. Developed, implemented, and evaluated compensation policies and programs (e.g., pay structures, performance-based pay). Provided advice on employee grievances and Claims involving pay and leave entitlements. Interpreted and applied pay rules and regulations to analyze employee and payroll information, and to identify and resolved pay-setting errors and discrepancies. Advised management, employees and union officials on work scheduling and flexibilities (including alternative work schedules) and premium pay entitlements associated with various work scheduling scenarios (e.g. overtime, night, and other pay). Managed payroll related data (e.g., new hires, adjustments, terminations). Served as a consultant providing guidance to managers and employees.

SKILL IN RECRUITMENT/STAFFING. Identified workforce requirements to achieve short and long-term goals in restructuring and workforce expansion. Assessed skill sets of internal workforce and external labor market to determine availability of qualified candidates. Developed and implemented selection procedures such as applicant tracking, interviewing, reference/background checking, and employment offers. Administered post-offer employment activities such as executing employment agreements, and completing I-9/e-verify process. Developed and implemented new hire orientation program, employee retention strategies, affirmative action plans (AAP), and records retention processes. Analyzed and evaluated current STAFFING concerns to identified and forecasted STAFFING. Provided outplacement services to employees terminated through attrition. Developed exit interview strategy to improve organizational culture and minimize exposure to litigation.

KNOWLEDGE OF HR INFORMATION SYSTEMS. Trained workforce on information systems security plans and policies. Developed policies and procedures to direct the appropriate use of electronic media and hardware (e.g. email, social media, website access). Knowledge of numerous HR software applications.

INSTRUCTION, PRESENTATIONS, AND BRIEFINGS: Led classes and small groups in classroom settings and webinars concerning topics such as relocation, time-management, goal setting, and responses to bullying in the workplace. Utilized written and oral communication skills to develop and deliver briefings, project papers, status/staff reports, and correspondence to managers to foster understanding and acceptance of findings and recommendations.

KEY ACCOMPLISHMENTS:

- Lowered health care renewal costs by approx. $175K for the 2010/2011 plan year by moving from a fully insured plan to a partially self-funded plan.
- Prepared organization's Affirmative Action Plan, for the 2009/2010 plan year; communicated results and goals to management.
- Reduced sporadic and random hiring by implementing a hiring process according to the Office of Federal Contract Compliance Programs (OFCCP) procedures.
- Created, implemented, and trained managers on anti-bullying policy, reducing number of organization-wide bullying complaints.

HUMAN RESOURCES MANAGER	02/2008 - 08/2009
J.R. Simplot	Salary: $75,000.00/Year
Grand Forks, ND United States	Hours per week: 50

Supervisor: David Skyler (777-777-7777)
Okay to contact this Supervisor: Yes

[Company is diverse, privately held agribusiness and food processing company - one of the world's largest food processors and one of the nation's largest beef cattle producers]

SUPERVISOR: Managed seven-person human resources team providing support for 400 employees across recruitment, hiring, EMPLOYEE RELATIONS, payroll and benefits, workers' compensation, and unemployment functions. Ensured all HR activities were compliant with applicable federal laws and regulations.

STRATEGIC PLANNING: Established STRATEGIC relationships with key organization individuals to assist in achieving the organization's STRATEGIC goals and objectives. Provided consultation and assistance to management team on complex and controversial conduct-related issues. Established objectives, procedures and plans that met both long- and short-range goals. Involved in consensus building, negotiating, coalition building, and conflict resolution techniques to interact appropriately in highly charged situations. Participated in disaster response exercises carried out by the organization, which resulted in a quicker response time in emergency situations. Prepared cost analysis, gathered data, and coordinated across multiple departments to craft request for proposal (RFP) to support manpower increases in specific positions. Skilled in collecting, evaluating, and disseminating information. Able to recognize strengths and weaknesses of programs to establish change initiative.

KEY ACCOMPLISHMENTS:
- Assisted in the implementation of organization's casualty/disaster response plan, which minimized the organization's exposure to liability in the event a loss or injury occurs.
- Facilitated site succession planning; ensured seamless progress during periods of change.

EDUCATION:

Human Resources Certificate 12/2006
Human Resources Certification Institute
Alexandria, VA United States
Major: Professional Human Resources (PHR)
Relevant Coursework:
Business Management and Strategy, Workforce Planning and Employment, Human Resources Development
Compensation and Benefits, Employee and Labor Relations, Risk Management

Master's Degree 04/2004
Troy State University, Alamogordo (Holloman AFB), NM United States
GPA: 3.9 of a maximum 4.0
Major: Management Minor: Human Resources

Bachelor's Degree 12/2002
University of Maryland University College, Ramstein, Germany
Major: Information Systems Management

SPECIALIZED TRAINING:

Boots to Business (SBA - 2012)
Transition Assistance Program (Military and Family Support Center - 2012)
Military Families in Transition (Zeiders/CNIC - 2012)
CIAC Confidentiality (Zeiders - 2012)
CIAC Orientation Conference (Navy - 2012)
Human Resources and The Law (National Seminars - 2011)

CERTIFICATION
Professional Human Resources (PHR) Certificate, Human Resources Certification Institute (2006)
Society of Human Resources Management (SHRM) - General Member
Human Resources Association for the National Capital Area (HRA-NCA) - General Member

COMPUTER SKILLS:

Proficient in use of most major computer systems, spreadsheet applications, presentation applications, and word processing applications, including but not limited to: MS Word, PowerPoint, Excel, and Internet Explorer. Expertise with HR applications including: PeopleSoft, JDE, SAP, DelTek, BalanceAAP.

If you are a Wounded Warrior, it can be tricky to figure out how to write about your recovery and rehabilitation time in your federal resume. Because each individual utilizes the Wounded Warrior Program in different ways, here are five suggestions on how to include your program activities in your federal resume.

1. Include a Short Description

WORK HISTORY:

USMC Wounded Warrior Regiment, West, Camp Pendleton, CA (Feb. 2013 to April 2014) Active Duty, E-5. Completed one year of medical, rehabilitative recovery, reconditioning, counseling and transition training in order to achieve wellness. Achieved a level of success to seek transition into civilian life.

2. Show Education and Training

PROFESSIONAL EXPERIENCE

WOUNDED WARRIOR, E-5	**09/2011-Present**
Warrior Transition Unit, Ft. Belvoir, VA	Salary: $71,416
Supervisor: SSgt Herbie Polo, 555-555-5555, may contact	40 hours/week

Undergoing intensive regimen of medical treatment and physical rehabilitation after suffering service-connected injuries in Iraq, 07/2011. Actively transitioning to civilian life, including by:

- **Earned cum laude Associate of Science Degree** in General Studies, 2012. Relevant courses: Principles of Microeconomics; Introduction to Business; Introduction to Computer Applications and Concepts; Math for Liberal Arts; Intercultural Communication.
- **Earned Access Data Certified Examiner**, 04/2013; completed 40-hour Digital Forensics course.
- **Completed additional Northern Virginia Community College course:** Introduction to Geospatial Imaging, 2013.
- **Developing knowledge** of Federal civilian employment process, including resume writing, skills translation, job series, application processes, and available employment resources.

3. Include Internships

USMC Wounded Warrior Regiment, West (12/2013 to present)
Active Duty, E-5, Camp Pendleton, CA

- Completed one year of medical, rehabilitative recovery, reconditioning, counseling and transition training in order to achieve wellness. Achieved a level of success to seek transition into civilian life.

- Successfully completed 3 internships while balancing work schedule with medical appointments and clinic visits (physical therapy sessions, and prosthetic related appointments).

HR Intern (September 2013–November 2013)
TriCare, San Diego, CA

SUPPORT HR ACTIVITIES: Attended and contributed to strategy meetings in an effort to refine the existing internship program. Worked closely with the Diversity and Inclusion Manager to share ideas and exchange program information.

Office Clerk/Intern (August 2013–October 2013)
Congressman Clark Kent's Office, San Diego, CA

REPORT GENERATION AND ADMINISTRATIVE SUPPORT: Created and maintained calendars; identifying and resolving any potential scheduling conflicts.

Talent Acquisition & Development Military Program Intern (April 2013–July 2013)
Genuine Education, San Diego, CA

4. Highlight Transition Skills Training

USCG Wounded Warrior, E-5   09/2013 – Present
Walter Reed National Military Medical Center   Salary: $71.416
Bethesda, Maryland   40 hours / week

WOUNDED WARRIOR REGIMENT: Participate in the Wounded Warrior Regiment which provides and facilitates assistance to wounded, ill, and injured military attached to or in support of USCG units, and their family members in order to assist them as they return to duty or transition to civilian life.

TRANSITION SKILLS DEVELOPMENT: Through comprehensive web-based employment toolbox, learn about: resume writing, skills translation, networking; transition courses; job placement; vocational rehabilitation; and specific guidance through the employment process by providing a range of employment resources and referral information.

KEY ACCOMPLISHMENTS: Learning how to strengthen myself from the inside out through special programs which show skills in how to improve overall self-esteem, self-confidence, and self-worth. Fully participate in: leadership, mentorship, lines of operation, individual and unit athletics, and community service events and activities.

REASON FOR LEAVING: Regained strength and abilities to return to work and life after the military. Transition date is December 31, 2013. I will be relocating to Bethesda, MD and separating from the USCG as an E-5 seeking a new career in Investigative Support Services. I am flexible about the location of my next employment. I am seeking a full-time position.

STEP 6

FOOD SERVICE SPECIALIST

Dynamic and hard-working food service professional with extensive experience in preparing and serving food, workplace sanitation, menu planning, and customer service. Proven team builder who exhibits decisiveness and leadership under pressure. Demonstrated ability to prioritize tasks and meet deadlines. Excellent public speaking and interpersonal skills. Proven customer service skills with diverse customers. Experience working as a Food Service Specialist for the United States Marine Corps. ***Currently in the Wounded Warrior Transition Program, NIH (08/2013 – Present).***

CAREER HISTORY AND HIGHLIGHTS

United States Marine Corps -
2012 – 2013
12th Marine Chow Hall
Camp Hansen, Okinawa, Japan
■ <u>Food Service Specialist</u>
- Procured, prepared, stored and distributed food for troop consumption.
- Oversaw menu and recipe planning; meal preparation and serving; sanitation; operation and management of facilities and personnel; training; and accounting and reporting functions for garrison and field operations.
- Handled the funding, requisitioning, purchasing, receiving, and accounting for sustenance supplies.
- Provided quality assurance surveillance procedures for food processing, mess hall operations, and storage facilities.

Pursuing Passion Led to Success

"A Wounded Warrior wanted to go into IT, but it wasn't his passion. He was just chasing the dollar. I asked him what he really enjoyed and had experience in. He told me it was dog training. There was a vacancy for that, and he got the job.

"By looking into their passion, the Wounded Warrior can end up doing something that they really enjoy doing. They can stay in the occupation for years to come, because they have a passion for it."

-- *Dennis Eley, MBA, Regional Wounded Warrior Coordinator at the OCHR San Diego Operations Center*

Targets: Human Resources Specialist & Management Training / Administrative Specialist

TORAN COLE

MOS: Infantry / Rifleman, MOS 0311

RECOMMENDED OCCUPATIONAL SERIES:

*   Administrative Specialist (0301)
*   Human Resources Specialist (0500)

RECOMMENDED TARGET GRADE LEVEL: GS - 7

HUMAN RESOURCES SPECIALIST - KEYWORDS

*   Internship development
*   Recruitment and placement
*   Employee relations
*   Report generation and administrative support
*   Hr program administration and support functions
*   Recruitment acumen and hr functions
*   Training, leadership
*   Team leader and coach
*   Communications

MANAGEMENT TRAINING / ADMINISTRATIVE SPECIALIST – KEYWORDS

*   Negotiations
*   Building coalitions
*   Partnerships
*   Team building / team leader
*   Coach and mentor
*   Trainer
*   Communications
*   Representative

Toran Cole

San Diego, CA 92102

703.555.1212

http://www.linkedin.com/in/torancole/

torancole@gmail.com

Leader | Military Professional | Program Developer

- Assisted in the development of the military internship program from the ground up and selected to meet with the CEO to discuss the program.
- Led and was responsible for 12+ marines on multiple deployments. Seven were promoted to the next rank.
- Through my dedication and determination earned multiple medals and letters of appreciation.

Clearance:

Inactive Top Secret Security Clearance (2008-2011)

Education:

Georgetown University, Washington D.C

BA in Business Administration, 2008

Experience:

CareFirst   **Sep 2013- Nov 2013**

HR Intern
- Worked with the Diversity & Inclusion Manager to gain more skills & insight in HR.
- Collaborated and provided ideas to for the internship program moving forward.
- Developed relationships and knowledge with all departments to help and give new ideas.
- Assisted with onboarding, scheduling interviews, and resume screening.
- Participated with phone interviews.
- Worked with all Microsoft Office programs such as PowerPoint, Word.

Congressman Jean Hunter's Office   **Aug 2013- Oct 2013**

Office Clerk- Intern

- Assisted the VA Liaison with helping constituents with issues or concerns.
- Provided excellent customer service to interested parties via phone.
- Created written documents for the community and nonprofit organizations such as Boy Scouts of American and The Boys and Girls Club.
- Organized mail that will be delivered to the appropriate departments.

Openpoint Education   **April 2013 - July 2013**

Talent Acquisition & Development Military Program Intern

- Assisted in the development of the military internship program.
- Developed professional development trainings such as business communications, professionalism, and interview 101.
- Created, organized and updated Power Point presentations and handouts for interns.
- Selected to meet with CEO of Bridgepoint Education to discuss Military Program initiatives.

Targets: Human Resources Specialist & Management Training / Administrative Specialist

- Exposure to social platforms and best practices in utilizing sources such as LinkedIn.
- Attended career fair and networking function while representing the organization.
- Worked and trained in using Microsoft Office programs, to include Excel, Word, and PowerPoint.

United States Marine Corps   **2007–present**

Sergeant

- Led combat operations and managed teams of 12+ marines, 7 promoted to Lance Corporal and Corporal Rank.
- Developed report with local populous in order to establish governance.
- Built strong working relationships with various communities to negotiate repairs, materials, and influence the local populous.
- Helping influence wounded marines to strive to be active in the communities by networking, and trying to give them the tools to be successful with job searching.

Lance Corporal

- Selected to work at the White House on Presidential security detail.
- Managed tasks associated with allocation of Marines for events and trips.
- Coordinated with Marine Corps and Secret Service – give Plan of Action.
- Successfully completed in upwards of 3 trips.
- Established communication lines for the President and other cabinet members.

Recognition and Awards:

- Successfully completed 2 deployments 2007 & 2011
- Letters of Appreciation for exemplary duty, 2008
- Afghanistan Campaign Medal, 2009 & 2011
- Good Conduct Medal 2010 & 2013
- Navy and Marine Corps Achievement Medal w/ V- for valor, 2011
- Purple Heart, 2011
- Combat Action Ribbon, 2011

The
Resume Place

11-Point Federal Resume Checksheet^{SM}

Your Name:
Your target job series or job title:
Your target grade level:

Toran Cole
Human Resources Specialist
GS-7

LENGTH: Is the resume 3 to 5 pages in length? *Too short in terms of matching a federal job announcement; missing details of the military chronology.*

ACCOMPLISHMENTS: Are accomplishments included for the last position or the most relevant position? *No*

FORMAT: Is the resume in the Outline Format? *The format is Private Industry Resume*

TYPEFONT: Is it easy to see keywords, either in ALL CAPS or boldface? *No*

KEYWORDS: Does the resume have keywords from a particular occupational series? *Keywords do not stand out.*

ONE YEAR SPECIALIZED EXPERIENCE: Is this clearly included in the resume? *Maybe*

10 YEARS EXPERIENCE: Does the resume focus on the last 10 years? *Yes*

RECENT AND RELEVANT: Does the resume feature recent and relevant for the target occupational series / job? The Internships are recent and relevant - *YES*

MONTH, YEAR AND HOURS PER WEEK: Are these included for the last 10 years? *No*

SALARY: Is salary information in the resume for positions in the last 10 years? *No*

TARGETING TOWARD AN OCCUPATIONAL SERIES: Is the resume targeted toward an occupational series with the correct keywords? *Not at all.*

A sample blank 11-Point Federal Resume
Checksheet is available on page 121.

This federal resume is in the USAJOBS Builder and is organized by reverse chronology. There are a lot of details that are mandatory with the USAJOBS builder, such as street addresses and zip codes for each Work Experience section. This USAJOBS builder resume is in the Outline Format with Keywords and Accomplishments.

Toran Cole

1223 San Diego Lane
San Diego, CA 92102 US
Mobile: 7777777777
Email: torancole@comcast.net

Availability: **Job Type:** Permanent
                           Work Schedule: Full-Time

Desired locations: United States - CA - San Diego
                              United States - CA - San Diego County

---

Work Experience: **USMC Wounded Warrior Regiment West**
Camp Pendleton, CA 92055 United States

12/2012 - 02/2014
Hours per week: 80
Wounded Warrior
Duties, Accomplishments and Related Skills:
Sergeant and Lance Corporal. Completed one year intensive program of medical, rehabilitative recovery, reconditioning, counseling and transition training in order to recover from near-fatal battle injury. Successfully completed three competitive internships while balancing work schedule with medical appointments and clinic visits. Achieved a level of success to transition to civilian workforce. Recipient of the Purple Heart, 2011.

Completed Three Human Resources Internships during this time. See more details below.
HR Intern - CareFusion
Office Clerk / Intern - Congressman Duncan Hunter's Office
Talent Acquisition & Development Military Program Intern - Bridgepoint Education

Supervisor: Dennis Ely (410 744 4324)
Okay to contact this Supervisor: Yes

United States Marine Corps
Camp Pendleton, CA 92055 United States

01/2009 - 02/2014
Hours per week: 40
Sergeant and Lance Corporal - Infantryman
Duties, Accomplishments and Related Skills:
Sergeant and Lance Corporal (2007–2014) Medically Retired, Feb. 2014
United States Marine Corps, San Diego, CA
Hours: 40 hours per week.

June 2009 – 7 months, Infantry, 3rd Battalion, 6th Marines Regiment, Marjah, Afghanistan

2007 to 2008 – Lance Corporal, White House Communications Officer

WHITE HOUSE AND MARINE CORPS LIAISON: Briefed the Secret Service on the security activities and communications of the U.S. Marines Corps during VIP visits and events. Coordinated all USMC infantry service. Held leadership decisions regarding assignments for trips and ensured the right skills. Rescheduled and augmented troops as needed in cooperation with Secret Service.

March 2011 – 12 months, Infantry, 1 Battalion, 5th Marines Regiment, Sangin, Afghanistan

LOCAL VILLAGE COMMUNICATIONS: Established local governance and re-established the Corps with the local villagers and U.S. Coalition Forces by sitting down, drinking tea and talking through an interpreter. We discussed infrastructure damages and provided claims cards for cash to repair property and compound wall damage that were caused by the U.S. from indirect fire and firefights.

TRAINING, LEADERSHIP AND PARTNER PATROLS: As a squad leader, developed a good rapport and partnered with the local uniform police and the National Army. Trained the local police to take the lead on some patrols and interdicted with their tactics. Staggered the local police with our Marines to demonstrate to the local villagers that the local police could lead operations.

TEAM LEADER AND COACH: Squad leader for 12 Marines with machine gun teams, demolition teams and a major battalion commander attached; essentially a total of 16 plus military members. Ensured Marines had mission essential gear and reported to the platoon commander. Supervised troubleshooting of gear and telecom equipment. Dealt with heat factors, keeping Marines' morale up with rest, breaks, time management, adequate sleep and at the same time ensuring security and the Marine mission.

Key Accomplishments:

TRAINING AND EDUCATION: To support the U.S. goal of Afghan self-sufficiency, I trained local Afghan soldiers according to global best practices. In particular, I communicated through an interpreter the importance of wearing uniforms, and carrying their weapons and gear to give the best possible protection.

I developed a rapport with the patrol base and talked to the Afghan commander through the interpreter, making it imperative that they wear the gear during the patrols. This practice ensured professionalism and protection of both Afghans and U.S. soldiers.

CareFusion
3750 Torrey View Court
San Diego, CA 92130 United States

09/2013 - 11/2013
Hours per week: 40
HR Intern
Duties, Accomplishments and Related Skills:
INTERNSHIP DURING WOUNDED WARRIOR TRANSITION

RECRUITMENT AND PLACEMENT: Screened resumes and reviewed application packages against position requirements. Oriented new hires and followed on-boarding procedures, including answering questions about their job roles and providing them with information pertaining to benefits, vacation time, and payroll.

EMPLOYEE RELATIONS: Provided support to supervisors, managers and employees on a variety of employee relations matters, to include resolving minor employee problems. Conducted research of pertinent guidance resolve disputes, and responded to inquiries regarding requirements of proposed actions.

ADVISOR: Advised on non-controversial issues, such as regulatory and procedural authorities relating to performance and performance ratings, disciplinary problems, employee dissatisfaction, indebtedness, work habits, and unexcused absences and provided guidance on alternatives and possible solutions. Explained provisions of employee benefits and services programs.

Key Accomplishments:

INTERNSHIP PROGRAM RE-DEVELOPMENT: Key member of strategy team working to refine the existing internship program for Wounded Warriors. Represented the voice of Wounded Warriors. Contributed to team meetings. Collaborated with the Diversity and

WOUNDED WARRIOR CASE STUDY: TORAN COLE
AFTER FEDERAL RESUME CONT.

Targets: Human Resources Specialist & Management Training / Administrative Specialist

Inclusion Manager to share ideas and exchange program information.

Congressman Duncan Hunter's Office
1611 Magnolia Ave
El Cajon, CA   92020 United States

08/2013 - 10/2013
Hours per week: 20
Office Clerk / Intern
Duties, Accomplishments and Related Skills:
INTERNSHIP DURING WOUNDED WARRIOR TRANSITION

REPORT GENERATION AND ADMINISTRATIVE SUPPORT: Created and maintained calendars, identifying and resolving any potential scheduling conflicts. Arranged and provided support for meetings which included preparing detailed agendas and meeting notices for both internal and external meeting participants.

COMMUNICATIONS: Ensured timely replies to all correspondence. Greeted the full range of visitors to the office. Answered phone calls; responded to routine inquiries or directed calls to appropriate subject matter specialist.

Key Accomplishments:

WRITER AND EDITOR: Drafted formal written documents on behalf of community and nonprofit organizations such as the Boy Scouts of America and The Boys and Girls Club.

Bridgepoint Education
13500 Evening Creek Dr N
San Diego, CA   92128 United States

04/2013 - 07/2013
Hours per week: 40
Talent Acquisition & Development Military Program Intern
Duties, Accomplishments and Related Skills:
INTERNSHIP DURING WOUNDED WARRIOR TRANSITION

HR PROGRAM ADMINISTRATION AND SUPPORT FUNCTIONS: Recruited interested individuals and provided them with program knowledge. Created, organized, and updated presentations and handouts for interested interns.

RECRUITMENT ACUMEN AND HR FUNCTIONS: Visited VA hospitals and attended career fairs at local military bases to deliver resume writing and interviewing workshops. Designed, developed, and implemented training classes to include Business Communications, Professionalism, and Interviewing 101.

Key Accomplishments:

SPEARHEADED THE DEVELOPMENT OF THE MILITARY INTERNSHIP PROGRAM: Bridgepoint Education is a national educational organization with nearly $1 billion in revenue each year. In keeping with President Obama's initiative to bring veterans into private industry positions, I developed a program aimed at integrating former military interns into pre-existing classes, workshops, and developmental trainings that were formerly available only to college interns.

Based on my work, I was selected to meet with the CEO of Bridgepoint Education to discuss Military Program initiatives.

Supervisor: Elizabeth Polo (677-777-7777)
Okay to contact this Supervisor: Yes

STEP 6

| **Education:** | **Georgetown University** Washington, DC   United States |
| | Bachelor's Degree 05/2008 |

Major: Business Administration
Relevant Coursework, Licenses and Certifications:
Attended college on full Basketball Scholarship. Traveled to Spain to consider a contract to play professional basketball for two years. Joined the USMC before the Professional Basketball career.

Job Related Training:

SKILLS:

MS Word®, Excel®, Outlook®; Internet research

Additional Information:

AWARDS:

+ Purple Heart, 2011
+ Successfully completed 2 deployments 2007 and 2011
+ Letters of Appreciation for exemplary duty, 2008
+ Afghanistan Campaign Medal, 2009, 2011
+ Good Conduct Medal 2010, 2013
+ Navy and Marine Corps Achievement Medal w/ V- for valor, 2011
+ Combat Action Ribbon, 2011

First collect all of the necessary information:

- Locate all of your written career papers, such as resumes, evaluations, and position descriptions.

- Find your list of training classes.

- Find or order your college transcripts.

- Find your DD-214 and other veteran's documents.

To get your first federal resume draft written:

- Start writing your first draft using the Classification Standards.

- Then, later you can tailor this draft to specific vacancy announcements.

> ### Links to the Classification Standards:
>
> **White Collar Positions:** www.opm.gov/fedclass/html/gsseries.asp
>
> **Trades, Craft, and Labor Positions:** www.opm.gov/fedclass/html/fwsdocs.asp

STEP 6

11-Point Federal Resume Checksheet^{SM}

LENGTH: Is the resume 3 to 5 pages in length?

ACCOMPLISHMENTS: Are accomplishments included for the last position or the most relevant position?

FORMAT: Is the resume in the Outline Format?

TYPEFONT: Is it easy to see keywords, either in ALL CAPS or boldface?

KEYWORDS: Does the resume have keywords from a particular occupational series?

ONE YEAR SPECIALIZED EXPERIENCE: Is this clearly included in the resume?

10 YEARS EXPERIENCE: Does the resume focus on the last 10 years?

RECENT AND RELEVANT: Does the resume feature recent and relevant for the target occupational series / job?

MONTH, YEAR AND HOURS PER WEEK: Are these included for the last 10 years?

SALARY: Is salary information in the resume for positions in the last 10 years?

TARGETING TOWARD AN OCCUPATIONAL SERIES: Is the resume targeted toward an occupational series with the correct keywords?

DO'S AND DON'TS FOR FEDERAL RESUME BUILDERS

DO!

Research Announcements

- ☐ Find at least one announcement that is correct for you.
- ☐ Analyze the keywords from duties, qualifications, and questions.
- ☐ Analyze the one year specialized experience that is important for your announcement.

Federal Resume Writing

- ☐ Make a list of accomplishments from your last two positions.
- ☐ Be sure to mention the types of customers you serve, and list the customers if you can.
- ☐ Write your first federal resume that will focus your resume toward one position.
- ☐ After you write ONE resume and target this toward ONE job series, you can write another resume version – with additional keywords.
- ☐ Count the characters for the builder, i.e., USAJOBS: 5,000 characters; DoD*ESS/AVUE: 4,000 characters for each work experience.
- ☐ Proofread and edit the resume – have a second person read the resume if you can.

Formatting for Resume Builders with the Outline Format

- ☐ Use ALL CAPS selectively with small paragraphs for your builder resume.
- ☐ The ALL CAPS keywords should match the keywords in the announcement.
- ☐ Paragraphs should be four to eight lines long.

Federal Resume Builders

- ☐ Copy and paste your resume into the various online builders.
- ☐ Preview the resume in the builder so you can correct any formatting problems.

DON'T!

- ☐ Don't write one federal resume and use it for all of your positions.
- ☐ Don't just submit your TAP GPS resume as your federal resume.
- ☐ Don't use too many acronyms.
- ☐ Don't copy and paste text straight from the announcement and your position description.
- ☐ Don't write your original resume in a builder (write the resume in software, then copy and paste into the builder).
- ☐ Don't write your federal resume in one paragraph (called the Big Block).
- ☐ Don't use a long list of bullets for your duties section.

- ☐ **RECOMMENDED: The Resume Builder is preferred by Federal Human Resources Specialists.**

- ☐ **UPLOAD TIP: If you upload a federal resume into USAJOBS, make sure you include all of the details that are marked as "required" in the USAJOBS Resume Builder, such as the month and year for employment start and end dates.**

STEP 6

Inventory Management Series, GS 2010

Inventory Management Series, GS-2010   TS-117 July 1992

The three primary functions that characterize the occupation are management, coordination, and control of inventory and systems of inventory management.

1. Inventory Management includes the integrated management and control of assigned items of material. The work involves a number of processes such as:

   (a) Requirements Determination - Planning for and determining current and future supply requirements to meet customer needs;

   (b) Material Distribution - Planning and determining the distribution and positioning of supplies among major supply stations, stock points, or using activities;

   (c) Procurement Authorization - Preparing recommendations and directives for the procurement of material, indicating the types of items, quantities, and at all times, the sources; and

   (d) Funds Management - Analyzing planned or scheduled material requirements and forecasts to determine categories and quantities of items, as well as funds required.

Public Affairs Series, GS-1035

Public affairs positions work in and contribute to a variety of functional programs. Much of this program knowledge is obtained from specialists in the functional program areas or through **review of agency developed material, interviewing program specialists, or reading professional and trade publications**. This series covers positions involving one or more of the following functions:

1. **design, plan, and direct or advise on the public affairs program** in an agency, or organization within an agency;
2. **develop and disseminate informational materials to the general public** or specialized target groups within a domestic or foreign setting;
3. provide information of particular value and **interest to agency employees**; U.S. Office of Personnel Management 2Public Affairs Series, GS-1035 TS-53 July 1981
4. **establish and maintain effective working relationships with all media**, both foreign and domestic, and develop and disseminate informational materials to pertinent publics through the media.

FACTOR EVALUATION SYSTEM (FES)

The Factor Evaluation System (FES) is part of the Classification Standards and includes nine factors that are part of most nonsupervisory GS positions. These descriptions are used for assigning grades under the GS system and are highly useful for improving your resume.

Look through the FES definitions in the Classification Standard for your target position. Where applicable, add the answers to the following key FES questions into your resume to dramatically improve your federal resume content.

KNOWLEDGE

- What knowledge do you have to help you do your job?

SUPERVISORY CONTROLS

- What kind of supervisory control do you have?
- Or do you work independently?

GUIDELINES USED

- What guidelines do you use to do your job?
- What laws, regulations or references?
- List all legislation, manuals, SOPs, policies, references

COMPLEXITY

- What is the scope of your position?

SCOPE & EFFECT

- Who do you talk to and work with?
- What is the scope of your work?
- Is it local, regional, worldwide?

PERSONAL CONTACTS AND PURPOSE OF CONTACTS

- Who are your customers?
- Are they nearby or do you work with them through email, etc.?
- How many customers do you support?

Before Resume: WITHOUT THE FES INFORMATION

Administrative Assistant (40 hrs per wk) (Massachusetts Air National Guard) Jan 08 – Present. Provide administrative support to the Chief of Staff (Massachusetts Air National Guard). Provide reports to queries on personnel matters utilizing data systems RCAS and IPERMS. Track suspense's, Executive Summaries, correspondence, briefings, and investigations utilizing an electronic log system. Review Executive Summaries for content, format, and administrative errors. Maintain Payroll Worksheets for 35 personnel monitoring hours worked and vacations taken, and provide summary reports to supervisors and finance personnel. Manage Moral and Welfare fund requests for Massachusetts National Guard units by reviewing requests for legality, administrative correctness, submitting the paperwork to the State Military Department, and coordinating issuance of checks. Monitor the Chief of Staff's calendar for appointments and events. Assist in developing/mentoring new personnel both enlisted and officer with office procedures.

After Resume: WITH THE FES INFORMATION

ADMINISTRATIVE ASSISTANT (40 hrs per wk) (Mass. Air National Guard)
Assistant to the Chief of Staff who oversees 3,000 Mass. National Guard Soldiers. Work independently to support all administrative, personnel, correspondence and payroll administration for the director.

COMPLEX ADMINISTRATION: Highly skilled in supporting multiple battalion deployments and re-integration and readiness during and following the ending of Iraq and Afghanistan. ACCOMPLISHMENT: Improved support for deployed and emergency support for the guardsmen. Organized and coordinated efficient ceremonies and events. Managed paperwork for complex deployments.

IMPLEMENT THE NATIONAL GUARD TECHNICIAN HANDBOOK. Implement and administer "The Technician Act of 1968", Public Law 90-486, for all support services for Reserves and Active duty personnel.

REPORTS AND DATABASE ADMINISTRATION AND COMPUTER SKILLS. Produce reports to queries on personnel matters utilizing data systems RCAS and IPERMS. Track suspenses, Executive Summaries, correspondence, briefings, and investigations utilizing an electronic log system.

CUSTOMER SERVICES FOR THE GUARD PERSONNEL: Manage Moral and Welfare fund requests for Massachusetts National Guard units by reviewing requests for legality and administrative correctness, submitting the paperwork to the State Military Department, and coordinating issuance of checks.

STEP 7

KSAs in the Federal Resume and Assessment Questionnaires

Have You Heard That KSAs Have Been Eliminated?

The traditional essays for the Knowledge, Skills, and Abilities (KSAs) narratives were eliminated. President Obama signed a memorandum to make immediate hiring reforms on May 11, 2010. See details at www.opm.gov/hiringreform/.

Though you may no longer need to write long, cumbersome essays as part of your federal job application, you STILL need to somehow demonstrate that you do in fact have the knowledge, skills, and abilities to perform the job duties described in the vacancy announcement. How to do this will depend on the application.

Then How Will You Demonstrate Your KSAs?

KSAs are currently being covered in four sections of the federal application:

1. KSA Accomplishments in the Resume
2. KSA narratives to support the Questionnaire (on occasion 4,000 to 8,000 characters)
3. KSAs in the multiple choice Questionnaire
4. KSAs as part of the Behavior-Based Interview

The Outline Format can include your KSAs easily with the ALL CAP HEADINGS. You can feature COMMUNICATIONS, WRITING, PROJECT MANAGEMENT, PLANNING AND COORDINATING and other KSAs or significant competencies as headings. The text under the headings can be examples from your accomplishment record that will demonstrate your KSAs.

Definitions

Knowledge: An organized body of information, usually of a factual or procedural nature, which, if applied, makes adequate performance on the job possible.

Skills: The proficient manual, verbal, or mental manipulation of data, people, or things. Observable, quantifiable, measureable.

Abilities: The power to perform an activity at the present time. Implied is a lack of discernible barriers, either physical or mental, to performing the activity.

Write your KSA answers by giving examples that demonstrate that particular knowledge, skill, or ability.

KSAs Are Also Known As:

- Selective Placement Factors
- Narrative Statements
- Essays
- Examples
- Quality Ranking Factors
- Key Elements
- Specialized Qualifications
- Technical & Managerial Qualifications

How KSAs Are Still Included in Your Application

KSAs are now included in the federal resume to demonstrate that you have the knowledge, skills, and abilities to perform the position and therefore are not rated and ranked per se. However, KSAs are also covered in the Questionnaire with most applications. The Questionnaires are scored based on your answers. So the prior rating and ranking of KSAs are now gone, but KSAs are actually still part of the federal application within the resume and the Questionnaire.

1 One excellent example per narrative will demonstrate that you have the knowledge, skills, and abilities for the position.

2 If possible and appropriate, use a different example in each accomplishment statement.

3 The typical length is 300 words or less.

WOW!

Write your accomplishment examples with specific details, including the challenge of the example and the results. 4

Spell out ALL acronyms. 5

6 Write in the first person. "I serve as a point-of-contact for all inquiries that come to our office."

7 Quantify your results and accomplishments.

8 Draw material from all parts of your life, including community service, volunteer projects, or training.

9 Limit your paragraphs to 6 to 8 lines long for readability.

10

Proofread your writing again and again.

Example #1: KSAs in the Resume

This example matches the federal resume to the required KSAs in the announcement.

Job Title: PUBLIC AFFAIRS SPECIALIST
Department: Department of the Army
Agency: U.S. Army Accession Command
Job Announcement Number: NEAJ12816501674933D

SPECIALIZED EXPERIENCE: Applicants must have one year of specialized experience at the GS-07 grade level to include the following areas: 1. Experience composing **written** documents such as newspaper articles/newsletters, news briefs, press releases, or feature articles for public media; 2. Experience utilizing current **social media networks** or video/digital formats to promote information, programs, events, or other newsworthy occurrences; and 3. Experience working with and **maintaining relationships** with individuals within and outside of an organization.

PARTNER/MANAGER   09/2010 - 02/2012

BaseCouponConnection.com, 47 Honeysuckle Lane, Fort Stewart, GA 31315
Salary: $2,160 per month, Hours per week: 70
Supervisor: Natalie Richards (Self), Phone: 912-463-3240, May contact.

(3) MARKETING PROGRAM FOR MILITARY FAMILIES WITH FAMILY MEMBER IN IRAQ. Developed, owned, managed and operated business that sold marketing contracts to local businesses. Marketed "Send It To Your Sweetie" program targeting free services to military families with members in Iraq for shipping, phone messages, and personal delivery of gifts for their loved ones. Met with base command to insure all regulations and policies were met.

- Accomplishment: Conceptualized a successful program for family members to send gifts and messages to military personnel. More than 2,500 messages were sent through this program in just six months. Sold business in less than 6 months for a substantial profit.

(1) COMMUNICATIONS. Wrote business plan and developed all aspects of advertising and marketing. Performed cold calls on business customers and followed up with written proposals. Created and delivered PowerPoint presentations to groups of various sizes. Organized and prepared mailings to families and businesses.

(2) WEBSITE DESIGN: Designed website and prepared spreadsheet to track monthly views and clicks. Due to volume of business, interviewed and hired 3 contractors to assist with billing, designing ads, and updating website.

EXAMPLE #2: Surprise Narrative KSAs in the Questionnaire

Sometimes after you complete the typical multiple-choice Questionnaire, you might be asked to write narratives to support your Questionnaire answers.

Questionnaire with Narrative Responses (4,000 characters)

Grade - 09 Questions

Based on your responses to the previous questions in this vacancy announcement, you've been forwarded to this additional phase. The following question(s) relate to the questions asked previously in this announcement. You can review your responses by using the Previous button. To successfully complete your application, please review and follow these instructions:

1. Respond to each question. If you do not have related experience, enter "N/A".

2. Your responses to all of the questions in this announcement must be substantiated by the information in your resume.

3. Select the "Next" button at the bottom of each screen to make sure that you have viewed and responded to all questions.

4. If you wish to save your responses and come back later to complete your application, enter placeholder text in any empty text fields, and click the "Next" button. For each web page, the system will time out after one hour of inactivity and your entries will be lost unless you select the "Next" button.

5. You can return to the vacancy and complete your application, but all information must be submitted by the closing date of the announcement.

6. Once you have responded to all questions, select the "Finish" button. The system requires that you select the "FINISH" button, or your application will not be saved; your application will be incomplete, and you will not be considered for this vacancy.

7. After selecting "FINISH" you will be returned to the USAJOBS site.

* 1. Describe your experience evaluating policies/implementing programs related to operation /maintenance of commercial buildings/leased space; analyzing the effectiveness/efficiency of building operations, equipment & automated systems; interacting with customers/stakeholders regarding building services to assess needs/recommend solutions; analyzing real property budgetary/financial data. Limit your response to 4,000 characters, which is approximately one typewritten page.
     Enter NA if Not Applicable.

4000 characters left (4000 character limit)

EXAMPLE #3: KSAs in the Questionnaire – Multiple Choice Answers

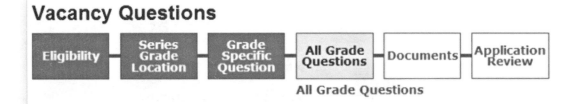

Vacancy Questions

| Eligibility | Series Grade Location | Grade Specific Question | All Grade Questions | Documents | Application Review |

All Grade Questions

Items marked with ***** are required.

All Grades Questions

Responses to the following questions will not be saved until you click the Next button. The system will time out after one hour unless you have clicked on the Next button to continue. It is recommended that you print the questions from the vacancy announcement and draft your responses before beginning the application process.

* 1. Do you have experience interacting directly with customers regarding building services and/or construction issues in order to assess customer needs and design solutions to meet those needs?

- ◉ Yes

- ○ No

* 2. Please indicate which of the following best describes your experience maintaining and nurturing customer relationships to enhance customer loyalty and retention.

- ○ I have not had experience performing this task.

- ○ I have performed similar or directly related tasks and my experience or training has equipped me to perform these functions successfully.

- ○ I have independently maintained and nurtured customer relationships to enhance customer loyalty and retention and only in unique or unusual situations did I require assistance or review by a supervisor or senior employee.

- ○ I have assisted a senior staff member in maintaining and nurturing customer relationships to enhance customer loyalty and retention.

- ◉ I am highly skilled at maintaining and nurturing customer relationships to enhance customer loyalty and retention. I have performed this task routinely and have conducted training in this area.

The Office of Personnel Management has a recommended format for writing KSAs and your accomplishments record in a story-telling format.

Introducing the Context, Challenge, Action, Result (CCAR) Model for writing better KSAs:

CONTEXT

The context should include the role you played in this example. Were you a team member, planner, organizer, facilitator, administrator, or coordinator? Also, include your job title at the time and the timeline of the project. You may want to note the name of the project or situation.

CHALLENGE

What was the specific problem that you faced that needed resolution? Describe the challenge of the situation. The problem could be disorganization in the office, new programs that needed to be implemented or supported, a change in management, a major project stalled, or a large conference or meeting being planned. The challenge can be difficult to write about. You can write the challenge last when you are drafting your KSAs.

ACTION

What did you do that made a difference? Did you change the way the office processed information, responded to customers, managed programs? What did you do?

RESULT

What difference did it make? Did this new action save dollars or time? Did it increase accountability and information? Did the team achieve its goals?

This CCAR story-telling format is also great for the Behavior-Based Interview. Write your accomplishment "stories" and prepare for the Interview Examination.

Please write a work or non-work related example to support a particular KSA or example required in an Assessment Questionnaire. Write your CCAR stories and accomplishments for the questionnaire examples, the Behavior-Based Interview, and a short version for your federal resume.

CONTEXT:

CHALLENGE:

ACTION:

1.

2.

3.

4.

RESULTS:

RECOGNITION/AWARD:

When KSAs are written on separate sheets of paper, the typical length is a 1/2 page for each, or 300 words or less. One or two examples can be written about to demonstrate your experience in this Knowledge, Skill, or Ability. These examples follow the CCAR story-telling formula.

It is still useful to write these KSA narratives for your Behavior-Based Interview to practice telling the story about your accomplishments.

Easy-to-use, Free KSA Accomplishment Builder:
  www.resume-place.com/ksa_builder/template/

---

1.   Knowledge of laws, rules, and regulations and ability to apply appropriate procedures in connection with payments, collections, or entitlements

Context: In my Administrative Assistant position in the Finance Office, Rota, Spain for 14 months, I HANDLED PAY REQUESTS and problem-solving from both civilian and military personnel. Maintained knowledge of military pay and leave regulations as stated in the Code of Military Personnel Regulations.

Challenge: I was a point of contact for soldiers returning from specialized training and deployments throughout CONUS and OCONUS.

Actions: I researched and resolved complex pay issues for soldiers and officers in support of deployment activities, travel, and repayment of expenses. I investigated databases for payment information, and followed up to ensure they were paid.

Results: Communicated with Defense Finance and Accounting Office Vendor representatives in Indianapolis to research problems and ensure payment. Was successful at establishing a contact who was responsive to my inquiries within 24 to 48 hours for numerous problem payment requests.

2. Ability to communicate orally.

Context: In my current position in Rota, Spain, I am the lead administrative assistant to the CO and XO for the U.S. Naval Base. I am experienced in representing the office with administrative information related to schedules, travel, and problem solving. I enjoy communicating with military personnel, family members, senior officers, and contractors.

An example of a particular experience where I demonstrated empathy and compassion in communications includes:

At Coronado NAS, I had the honor to be a volunteer administrative member of the first Warrior in Transition Program for the base.

Challenge: The major challenges were that this was the first organization of this type for Coronado and required interviewing and assessing the needs of the returning military from Iraq and Afghanistan and their family members.

Actions: I was trained to provide advocacy and services to family members to support special needs regarding health care services, critical medical services, and support for medical care. I communicated with military personnel and family members to refer services for medical care and assistance.

Results: The program is now established, and procedures and resources are set up for family members and military personnel who may be needing support from the Warrior in Transition Program. Coronado NAS has approximately 100 service members in the Warrior in Transition Program presently.

> "...allow individuals to apply for Federal employment by submitting resumes and cover letters or completing simple, plain language applications, and assess applicants using valid, reliable tools..."
>
> *The White House, Office of the Press Secretary, May 11, 2010*
> *Presidential Memorandum on Improving the Federal Recruitment and Hiring Process*

Cover letters are now officially part of the federal application!

Specialized Experience
Add a list of skills and experience that you can offer that matches the Specialized Experience in the announcement.

Passion and Interest in the Mission
Write about your interest in the mission of the agency or organization. If you know the mission and can speak about it in a sentence, you can stand out above your competition.

Letter of Interest
The cover letter IS a letter of interest. You are interested in the job. The cover letter is more than a transmittal. Take this opportunity to sell your special qualifications, certification, training, and mission-related experiences. This is another small writing test.

Adding or Uploading a Short Cover Letter into the Resume Builder
With USAJOBS, you can add the letter into Additional Information section. With Application Manager, you can upload your cover letter.

Special Considerations
You can mention your willingness to relocate, eligibility for non-competitive spouse appointments, veterans' preference, reasons for wanting to move, such as family, and other special interest items in the cover letter.

Why Hire Me?
Be sure to mention your best qualities (that match the announcement).

Compelling
Tell the reader why you are an excellent candidate and you believe in their mission.

Easy-to-use, free Cover Letter Builder:
www.resume-place.com/fedres_builder/cover_letter/

Be sure to include announcement qualifications in your cover letter, such as: providing assistance to senior specialists in the evaluation and analysis of training programs; assisting in the execution of training programs by carrying out specified portions or segments of specific projects (e.g., preparing and coordinating training requests, advertising upcoming training, maintaining training attendance data, arranging training spaces and locations, identifying training needs and informing staff of upcoming training classes); and identifying and recommending solutions to training problems and providing advice to staff on established methods and procedures.

MELODY ANN RICHARDS
2222 Alexandria Boulevard
Falls Church, VA 22043
Phone: 703-333-3333
Email: *melody.richards@army.mil*

US Department of State
Application Evaluation Branch
2401 E Street, NW
Washington, DC 20522-0108
ATTN: John Jones
RE: MISSION SUPPORT SPECIALIST (TRAINING), Annct No: 30303

Dear Mr. Jones:

Enclosed are my application materials for the Mission Support Specialist (Training Coordinator) within the Foreign Service Institute, Department of State.

I can offer the Foreign Service Institute the following training and program coordination skills:

- Evaluating and analyzing training programs and curriculum
- Coordinating training programs by professional instructors
- Managing training space, training equipment needs
- Managing registrations and attendance
- Identifying and recommending training solutions to individuals and managers
- Recommending training techniques to improve evaluations and customer satisfaction

One of my strongest assets as a training administrator is my ability to manage complex international courses and programs and resolve problems related to instructors, curriculum, and technology.

I am dedicated to helping to coordinate international training programs for Department of State and other foreign affairs agencies to assist employees transitioning from full-time government work due to retirement or involuntary separation. I am highly detailed and can offer diplomacy and tact in communicating with State Department professionals and Foreign Service Officers.

I am willing to travel if needed and am planning to relocate to the DC area next month. I am available for an interview at your convenience.

Sincerely,
MELODY ANN RICHARDS

STEP 8

Apply for Jobs with USAJOBS

Currently, there are many ways to apply for federal jobs. If you have both a paper federal resume and an electronic resume prepared, you should be ready to apply to all of the jobs in their various required formats. After you apply to a few of the announcements, you will get faster and be able to adjust your resume to fit the application requirements.

Read the "how to apply" instructions, because they could be different for each announcement. Get ready to copy and paste into builders, answer questions, write short essays, and fax or upload your DD-214 and transcripts. Apply a day early if possible to navigate the automated application systems.

Resume 1: MSW Veterans Administrati...
View | Edit | Duplicate | Delete
Status: Not Searchable
Make Searchable
Format: USAJOBS Resume
Source: Built with USAJOBS Resume Builder

Resume 2: IT Spec, Customer Service...
View | Edit | Duplicate | Delete
Status: Not Searchable
Make Searchable
Format: USAJOBS Resume
Source: Built with USAJOBS Resume Builder

Resume 3: IT Specialist Veteran JS ...
View | Edit | Duplicate | Delete
Status: Not Searchable
Make Searchable
Format: USAJOBS Resume
Source: Built with USAJOBS Resume Builder

Resume 4: Air Traffic Controller (T...
View | Edit | Duplicate | Delete
Status: Not Searchable
Make Searchable
Format: USAJOBS Resume
Source: Built with USAJOBS Resume Builder

[Build New Resume] [Upload New Resume]

You have created **4** of **5** possible resumes. You are able to upload and store **5** resumes to your My USAJOBS account.

Be patient and consider each job and agency separately. Your perseverance will pay off. Learn how to copy and paste quickly. Use the control-A (select all), control-C (copy), and control-V (paste) commands. This will speed up your copy and paste submissions.

On left: screenshot of Kathryn Troutman's USAJOBS resumes page.

Getting Started with USAJOBS

Use this getting started guide to set up your USAJOBS account and apply for federal jobs!

1. Logging In: Write Down Your Password!

Applicants routinely complain that they forget their password, which must include numbers, symbols, and letters. Make sure you link your account to a personal email, not a work email, so that you can access it at home.

2. Edit Your Profile: Answer Carefully!

The profile section of USAJOBS will pop up when you register or can be accessed by clicking on "Edit Profile" on the Main page.

You will be asked to enter Contact Information, Hiring Eligibility, Preferences, Demographic Information, and Account Information.

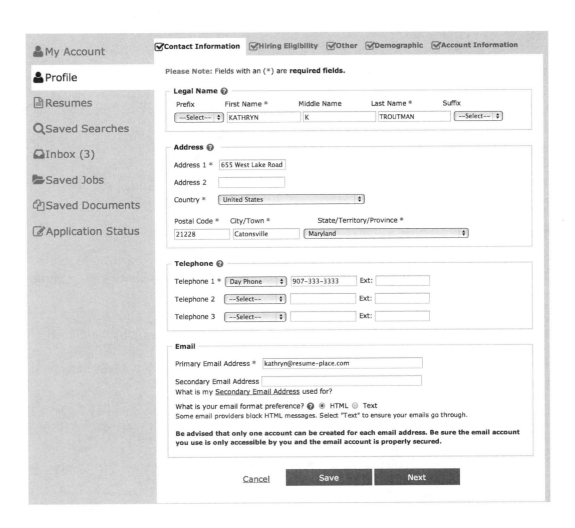

3. Contact Information

Be sure to enter an email address for your home, not work. In the event that you forget your password, the system may need to contact you via email for confirmation. You want to make sure you have listed an email address that you can always access.

Email

Primary Email Address *   kathryn@resume-place.com

Secondary Email Address
What is my Secondary Email Address used for?

What is your email format preference? ❓ ⦿ HTML ○ Text
Some email providers block HTML messages. Select "Text" to ensure your emails go through.

Be advised that only one account can be created for each email address. Be sure the email account you use is only accessible by you and the email account is properly secured.

---

4. Eligibility

Your answers to these questions can determine whether or not your resume and application ever make it to human resources. So, answer carefully.

U.S. Citizen: Most federal jobs require citizenship.

Selective Service: If you are a man, did you sign up for the draft? Many times you may not remember doing so, but it is a normal part of getting a driver's license, voting, etc.

Contractors do not have "reinstatement eligibility."

Current and Former Federal Employees: Select the appropriate answer regarding federal employment status and reinstatement eligibility. Also answer questions about your agency, organization, pay plan, series, and grade level/pay.

---

4. Please select the statement below which best reflects your federal employment status (if applicable). * ❓

○ I am not and have never been a federal civilian employee.

⦿ I am currently a federal civilian employee.

○ I am a former federal civilian employee with reinstatement eligibility.

○ I am a former federal civilian employee but do not have reinstatement eligibility.

- By which Federal agency and organization are you currently employed?

Select Department: | Department Of Homeland Security ▼ |

Select Agency: | Transportation Security Administration ▼ |

- Indicate the pay plan, series, grade level/pay band of the highest permanent graded position you ever held as a Federal Civilian Employee. (Question does not apply to members of the armed forces covered under Title 10.)

Pay Plan: | GS – General Schedule ▼ |

Occupational Series: | 0342 Support Services Administration ▼ |

Highest Pay Grade: | 09 |

5. Eligibility Documentation

Veterans

When claiming preference, veterans must provide a copy of their DD-214, Certificate of Release or Discharge from Active Duty, or other acceptable documentation.

Applicants claiming 10-point preference will need to submit Form SF-15, Application for 10-point veterans' preference. Ensure your documentation reflects the character of discharge.

If you do not upload your documentation, you will not be eligible for veterans' preference.

Federal Employees

If you are a current federal employee, you must upload your SF-50, or you will not be considered for jobs open only to current feds.

Veterans' Document Upload:

When claiming veterans' preference, preference eligibles must provide a copy of their DD 214, Certificate of Release or Discharge from Active Duty, or other acceptable documentation. Applicants claiming 10 point preference will need to submit an SF-15, Application for 10-point Veterans' Preference.

For current service members who have not yet been discharged, a certification letter of expected discharge or release from active duty within 120 days under honorable conditions is required at the time of application. Ensure your documentation reflects the character of discharge.

Document Title: [   ]

Document Type: ❓   Select Document:

| DD–214 ▼ | [Choose File] No file chosen

Files must be less than 3mb and can be in one of the following formats: GIF, JPG, JPEG, PNG, RTF, PDF, or Word (DOC or DOCX).

[Upload]   [Cancel]

6. Veterans' Preference

Veterans can select the preference type that applies to them. Veterans' Preference may also apply to spouses, widows and parents in some situations. If you think you will receive a disability rating, but have not received it yet, you must wait before selecting the 10 point category. You will need to provide paperwork to prove any disability rating. To determine your points, you can use this automated advisory system from the Department of Labor: http://www.dol.gov/elaws/vetspref.htm

Even if you are not eligible for preference, veterans may be eligible for other types of special hiring authorities if you served 3 years and received an honorable discharge.

---

3. Are you a Veteran of the U.S. Armed Forces or are you eligible for "derived" preference? *
   ● Yes   ○ No

   • Do you claim Veterans' Preference?

     ○ No, I do not claim Veterans' Preference

     ○ 0-point Sole Survivorship Preference (SSP)

     ○ 5-point preference based on active duty in the U.S. Armed Forces (TP)

     ○ 10-point preference based on a compensable service connected disability of at least 10% but less than 30% (CP)

     ○ 10-point preference based on a compensable service connected disability of 30% or more (CPS)

     ○ 10-point preference for non-compensable disability or Purple Heart (XP)

     ● 10-point preference based on widow/widower or mother of a deceased veteran, or spouse or mother of a disabled veteran (XP)

   • Are you a veteran who was separated from the armed forces under honorable conditions after completing an initial continuous tour of duty of at least 3 years (may have been released just short of 3 years)(VEOA)?
     ● Yes   ○ No

There are many government initiatives that give employment preference to specific and targeted segments of the population. The special hiring options include:

Veterans Recruitment Appointment (VRA): An excepted authority that allows agencies to appoint eligible veterans without competition if the veteran has received a campaign badge for service during a war or in a campaign or expedition; or is a disabled veteran; or has received an Armed Forces Service Medal for participation in a military operation; or is a recently separated veteran (within the last 3 years) and separated under honorable conditions. Appointments under this authority may be made at any grade level up to and including a GS-11 or equivalent. This is an excepted service appointment, which can be converted to competitive service after two years.

30% or More Disabled Veteran: A person who was separated under honorable conditions from active duty in the Armed Forces performed at any time and who has established the present existence of a service-connected disability rated at 30% or greater or is receiving compensation, disability retirement benefits, or pension because of a public statute administered by the Department of Veterans Affairs or a military department.

Disabled veterans who have completed a VA training program: A person who meets the definition of a disabled veteran and has successfully completed a program to receive training or work experience at VA.

Military Spouse: Military spouses are eligible under this authority if the active duty military spouse: 1) receives a Permanent Change of Station (PCS) move; 2) has a 100% disability rating; or 3) died while on active duty. Each of these categories has different eligibility criteria that must be met.

Certain Former Overseas Employees: A family member (which includes same-sex domestic partners) of a federal civilian employee or military member who has completed 52 weeks of service in a federal position overseas is eligible for appointment in the competitive service for a period of three years following the date of their return to the United States from the overseas area.

Schedule A Disabled Individuals with Intellectual Disabilities, Severe Physical Disabilities, or Psychiatric Disabilities may apply for non-competitive appointment through the Schedule A (5 C.F.R. 213.3102(u)) hiring authority. Documentation of the disability is required from a licensed medical professional; a licensed vocational rehabilitation specialist; or any federal, state, or District of Columbia agency or U.S. territory that issues or provides disability benefits.

VETERANS WHO ARE DISABLED SHOULD SELECT "SCHEDULE A DISABLED" IN ADDITION TO THEIR HIRING PREFERENCE IN QUESTION 4.

Special Hiring Options ❓

Select from among the special hiring authorities listed below for which you are eligible.
(Please note that agencies will require documentation of eligibility prior to your appointment.)

Identification of eligibility for any special hiring authority is entirely voluntary, and you will not be subject to any adverse treatment if you decline to provide it. If you do not wish to volunteer this information at this time, you may still choose to apply for jobs, as they are announced, under any of these special hiring authorities for which you are eligible. If you volunteer to provide information here about the special hiring authorities for which you believe you are eligible, then agencies who are searching for potential applicants to hire under one of these authorities may be able to locate your resume through USAJOBS and invite you to apply. Otherwise, this information will be retained in the USAJOBS database and not disclosed. For information on each of the special hiring options below, please review the definitions on our Special Hiring Options page.

- ☑ Veterans Recruitment Appointment (VRA)
- ☑ 30% or More Disabled Veteran
- ☑ Disabled veterans who have completed a VA training program
- ☑ Military Spouse
- ☐ Certain former overseas employees
- ☑ Schedule A Disabled

Cancel | Previous | Save | Next

---

8. Other

Applicants should choose carefully in this section because their answers will determine whether they are eligible later.

Are you willing to travel? If you say "No" you will be disqualified from a job, even if the amount of travel is very minimal.

What type of work are you willing to accept? Consider that more federal agencies are using "temp" and "term" jobs to fill positions when money is tight, or when the future is unknown. For example, many jobs that came out of the mortgage crisis were initially term jobs that eventually may become permanent.

If you accidentally apply for a "temp" or "term" job, but didn't click the button on this page, your application won't be read at all by human resources.

What type of work schedule are you willing to accept? Consider being flexible.

Select your desired work location(s). Select all of U.S. and if you apply for a job abroad, remember to come back and select that location as well.

If you only pick D.C., you might later be disqualified for a job in Baltimore.

9. Demographic

Your answers to this question are voluntary and do not affect whether or not you will be hired.

10. Personal Information

Write down your password! Also, you can choose to receive "Notification Alerts" on your application. This is important in case a job posting is pulled or re-announced.

Notification Settings

Notification Alerts enable you to stay informed of changes to your application status.

Select the items that you would like to be notified of via your primary email. You may edit your preferences and unsubscribe at any time.

- ☑ When jobs I have started an application for have closed.

- ☑ When jobs I have saved are scheduled to close in three calendar days.

- ☑ When the status of an application I've submitted changes.

Cancel | Previous | Save | Finish

---

11. My Account Main Page

Profile: Personal Information, Hiring Eligibility, Preferences, Demographic Information, and Account Information

Resumes: You can save up to five resumes in USAJOBS. That includes uploaded resumes and resumes built using the USAJOBS Resume Builder.

Saved Searches: Save your preferences for jobs you've searched in the past.

Saved Jobs: You can bookmark jobs you like.

Saved Documents: Your uploaded documents appear here. If you are using education to qualify for experience, you must upload your transcripts. They can be unofficial (HR will ask for official transcripts if you are hired).

Application Status: This section helps you track and follow up on your application and determine if you've actually applied.

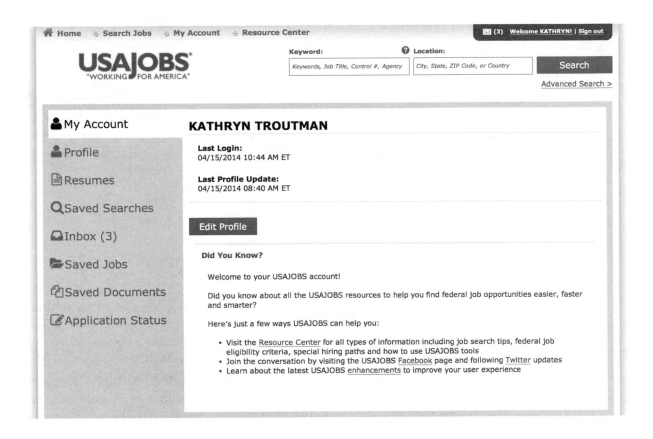

12. Resume Builder

Using the USAJOBS Resume Builder increases the chances that you will apply correctly for a federal job. Candidates who miss critical information on their resume will not be considered.

Work Experience

❏ No formatting or special characters.

❏ Use ALL CAPS to highlight important words.

❏ Use small paragraphs to ensure readability.

❏ Jobs are listed strictly in chronological order.

❏ Drop jobs that are not recent or relevant. Human resources won't read past 15 years.

❏ Human Resources Specialists are looking for your "ONE YEAR SPECIALIZED EXPERIENCE." "One year" means 52 weeks, 40 hours per week. Locate this important section in each announcement.

❏ Ensure that all of your jobs and keywords are focused.

❏ Ensure human resources can qualify you by including salary.

❏ Education and non-paid experience can be listed as a job.

❏ If you are using education to qualify for your "one year specialized," you must include a copy of your transcripts.

❏ May we contact your supervisor? You may answer "no." It will not affect your application.

Education

❏ Applicants for jobs with "positive education requirements", e.g., accountants, must list their courses and include credit hours.

❏ Online degree programs must be accredited.

❏ Don't include your GPA unless it is 3.5 or above.

❏ If you are "overeducated," you might want to leave off some degree information, such as multiple Masters or a Ph.D. you don't use.

Other

❏ Job Related Training: Avoid the temptation to go overboard. Stick to recent and relevant training.

Additional Information:

❏ This section has 20,000 characters and could include anything.

❏ Some candidates use it for a "Professional Profile." Human resources probably won't read it, but the hiring official might.

References

❏ Two references are not required, but they are recommended. Job-related references are best.

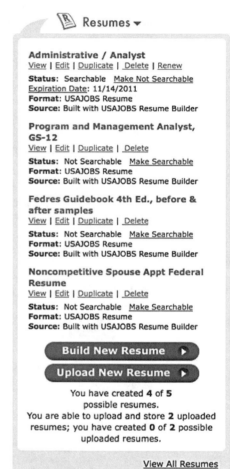

IMPORTANT TIP

The resume upload feature should only be used for one time and only for one application! Your uploaded resume might NOT get forwarded to the assessment questionnaire system. Also, the uploaded resume might not include all of the compliance details required by that agency. It is recommended to use the resume builder instead!

This automated system, run by USA Staffing, is frequently used in conjunction with USAJOBS, where https://applicationmanager.gov is the utility for administering the self-assessment and supplemental data questions. Application Manager is now run in conjunction with USAJOBS so that it is no longer necessary to have a separate Application Manager account.

When you select Apply Now on USAJOBS, you will then choose the resume to take with you to Application Manager.

Resume - Select one of your stored USAJOBS resumes to send :
- ○ MSW Veterans Administration
- ○ IT Spec, Customer Service, GS-2210-11
- ○ IT Specialist Veteran JS Guide 5th
- ○ Air Traffic Controller (Trainee)
- ○ Resume for CDP

Attachment(s) - Select one or more of your Saved Documents to send (or first Save Job and Upload Documents). :
- ☐ COVER (Class Notes Fedres Writing)
- ☐ COVER (ED Cover Letter)

Fields below with an asterisks (*) are required.

* ☐ I have previewed my resume . The selected document includes the information I wish to provide with this application.

☐ Allow me to attach demographic information to the application. Review or update your demographic information.

* ☐ I certify, to the best of my knowledge and belief, all the information submitted by me with my application for employment is true, complete, and made in good faith, and that I have truthfully and accurately represented my work experience, knowledge, skills, abilities and education (degrees, accomplishments, etc.). I understand that the information provided may be investigated. I understand that misrepresenting my experience or education, or providing false or fraudulent information in or with my application may be grounds for not hiring me or for firing me after I begin work. I also understand that false or fraudulent statements may be punishable by fine or imprisonment (18 U.S.C. 1001).

[Apply for this position now!] [Cancel]

If the agency is using Application Manager as the Automated Recruitment System for their questionnaire and document collection, you will be taken to this site automatically from USAJOBS.

1. You can utilize the USAJOBS resume or upload another resume and other pertinent application documents, as well as other information that they might request—last evaluation, DD-214 (veterans), and transcripts, for example.

2. You will complete the self-assessment questions. Follow all steps through "SUBMIT MY ANSWERS," or your application will not be submitted.

Ready to Submit?

[Submit My Answers]

Each agency can select their Automated Recruitment System (ARS) for managing and tracking their applicants.

The applicant questionnaires are basically similar amongst the different systems and will usually include multiple choice and self-assessment style questions.

Carefully follow the directions!

See examples of different automated recruitment systems on these two pages.

Monster.com (Transportation Security Administration)

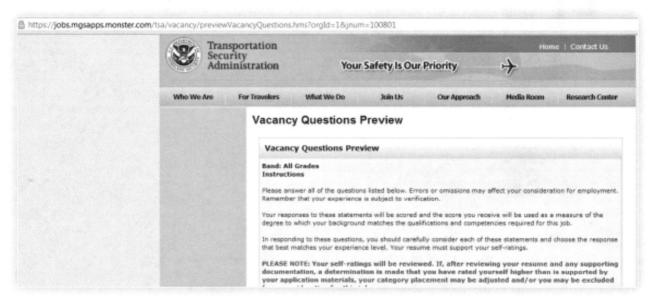

USAStaffing (U.S. Customs and Border Protection)

CareerConnector (U.S. Department of Agriculture)

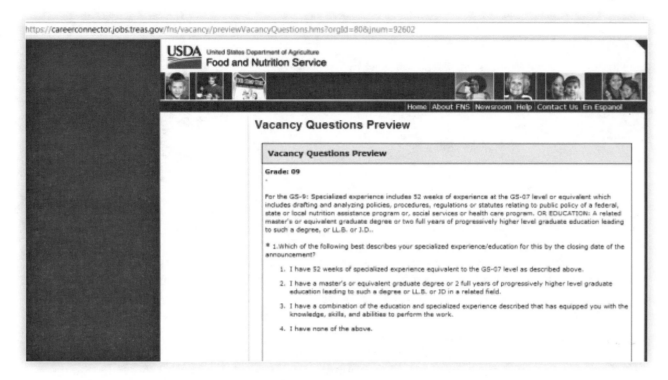

NTIS.gov (U.S. Forest Service)

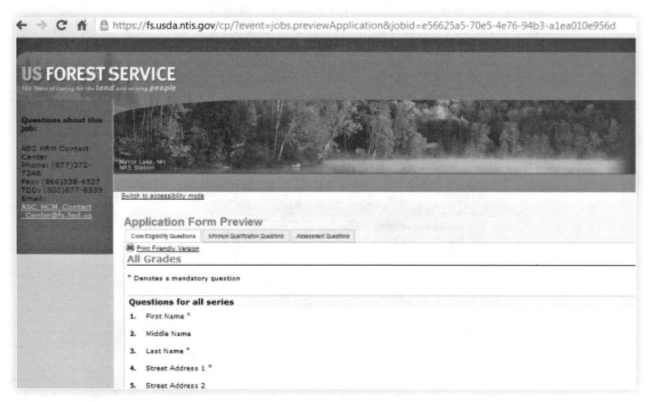

STEP 9

Track and Follow Up on Your Applications

Learn how to follow up and manage your federal job search campaign. Since the automated systems are so popular with federal agencies now, many of them include an automated reply system, as well as an online page where you can check the status of your applications. Some people can even read the notice, "you have been offered the position" online.

A federal job applicant can follow up by phone on some job announcements as well. Those that include a name and phone number make follow-up possible. It's important to keep track of your applications. Keep the announcements, and follow up on those that include a name and phone number after four to six weeks.

How Long Does It Take to Fill a Federal Job?

The current goal for length of time to fill a federal vacancy is 45 days from the date of posting job announcement. However, in our experience, the curent average time seems to be more around the range of 90 to 120 days.

How People Are Hired: The Competitive Process

Identify Job and Assessments

Recruit and Announce Job

Accept and Review Applications

Assess Applicants

Certify Eligibles

Select

USAJOBS & Application Manager

Most of the automated application systems have tracking systems where you can check the status of your application. Be sure to check your status regularly. Save your user name and password for each builder.

Find Out Your Application Score Online

You can check on the status of your applications in both USAJOBS and Application Manager. Look for the Notification of Results (NOR), which will tell you the outcome of your application.

Emails from Human Resources

The May 11, 2010 Presidential Memorandum issued by the White House on *Improving the Federal Recruitment and Hiring Process* recommends the use of emails by HR specialists to inform applicants about the status of their application and the vacancy announcement. If you receive an email from the HR specialist concerning your qualifications for the position and you can't understand the email, just write back or call to get clarification of the email.

Sample Telephone Message Script

"Hello, I'm Kathryn Troutman. I'm calling regarding my application submitted for announcement number 10505 for Writer-Editor, GS-12. The closing date was 3/31 and I'm checking on the status of the recruitment. I can be reached at 410-744-4324 from 9 until 5, Monday through Friday, Eastern Standard Time. If you get voicemail, you can leave a message regarding the position. Thank you for your time. I look forward to your information."

Emailing the HR Representative

If there is an email address on the announcement, you could try contacting the human resources specialist by email. You can contact the HR specialist to check on the status of your applications and find out your application score if this information is not posted online. Here is a sample letter:

Subject line: Status of announcement 10101

Dear Ms. Jones,

I submitted my Federal resume, KSAs, and evaluation for the position of Writer-Editor, announcement no. 10101 on Dec. 22 by USPS. I'd like to check the status of my application and the recruitment, please.

Is it still open and was I found qualified? Thank you very much for your time.

Sincerely,

Kathryn Troutman, SSN: 000-00-0000

Daytime phone: 410-744-4324 (M-F EST) messages okay

What Happens to Your Application?

Category Rating is the ranking and selection process that is now mandatory under Presidential Memorandum, May 11, 2010. We are currently in a time of transition between the previous point system (rate and rank) and the new category rating system.

No More Scores

Under category rating, there is no disclosure of crediting plans (points) and/or rating schedules with scoring keys.

Three Buckets of Applicants

All of the applications are evaluated and sorted into three groups, which we like to call buckets.

- **Best Qualified** – This is the <u>only</u> group that will get Referred to the Supervisor.

- **Well-Qualified** – This group will <u>not</u> be referred.

- **Qualified** – This group will <u>not</u> be referred.

Minimum Requirements

All applicants who meet the basic qualification requirements established for the position are ranked by being assigned to the appropriate quality category based upon the job-related assessment tool(s) – the questionnaire!

"If you're not in the top bucket, you're not in the game!"

– Kathryn Troutman

STEP 9

The following steps demonstrate how veterans' preference is applied in category rating.

1. Applicants are rated.

The following appplicant list was collected from a **US Citizen** announcement. Their applications are evaluated and they are given one of three ratings, such as Good, Better, and Best.

2. Additional points are assigned based on type of veterans' preference.

- CPS: disability of 30% or more (10 points)
- CP: disability of at least 10% but less than 30% (10 points)
- TP: served at specific time and not disabled (5 points)
- XP: less than 10% disability or derived preference for certain family members (10 points)

> Veterans' preference rules apply to vacancy announcements that use Category Rating to assess candidates and are open at all U.S. Citizens. Veterans' preference rules do not apply in internal merit promotion announcements.

3. CPS and CP rise to the top of the highest quality category.

Qualified preference eligibles with a compensable service-connected disability of 30% or more (CPS) and those with a compensable service-connected disability of more than 10% but less than 30% (CP) are placed at the top of the highest quality category.

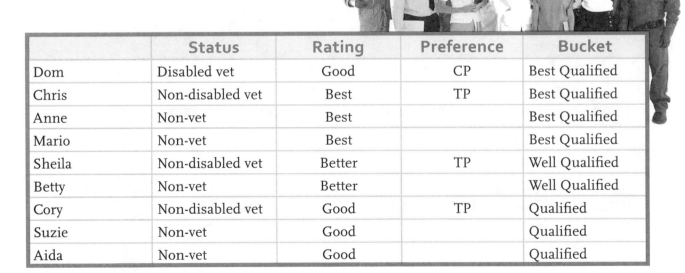

	Status	Rating	Preference	Bucket
Dom	Disabled vet	Good	CP	Best Qualified
Chris	Non-disabled vet	Best	TP	Best Qualified
Anne	Non-vet	Best		Best Qualified
Mario	Non-vet	Best		Best Qualified
Sheila	Non-disabled vet	Better	TP	Well Qualified
Betty	Non-vet	Better		Well Qualified
Cory	Non-disabled vet	Good	TP	Qualified
Suzie	Non-vet	Good		Qualified
Aida	Non-vet	Good		Qualified

This sample pool of applicants demonstrates how the CP applicant rose to the top of the group even though the rating for that particular applicant was good and not best.

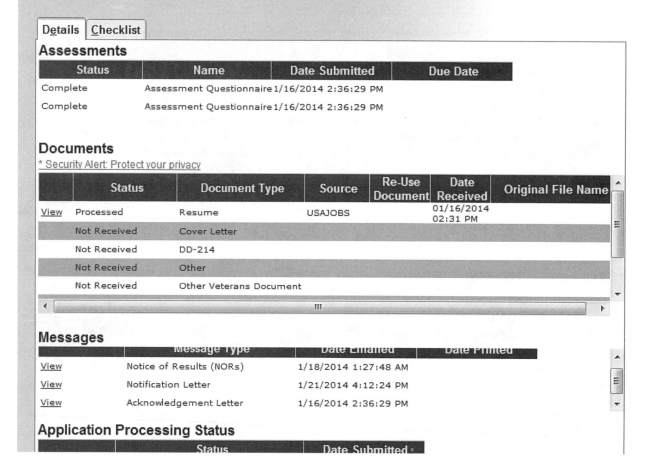

Application Package Status: See Details Tab

Job Title: INVENTORY MANAGEMENT SPECIALIST

Vacancy Identification Number: 1026916

Announcement Number: 9S-TRANS-1026916-038368-MAF

USAJOBS Control Number: 358913500

Applicant: KATHRYN K TROUTMAN

Closing Date: Thursday, January 16, 2014

Contact: AFPC RSC - (800)525-0102

Change My Answers · Add Documents · Update Biographic Information · View/Print My Answers

Most information below pertains to the most recent version of your Application Package. (Explain This.)

Notice to Applicants: Please ensure you keep copies of all documents you uploaded or faxed, including your resume, as well as any notifications sent to you. They will be deleted from the system after 3 years of the closing date of the announcement.

Details | Checklist

Assessments

Status	Name	Date Submitted	Due Date
Complete	Assessment Questionnaire	1/16/2014 2:36:29 PM	
Complete	Assessment Questionnaire	1/16/2014 2:36:29 PM	

Documents

* Security Alert: Protect your privacy

	Status	Document Type	Source	Re-Use Document	Date Received	Original File Name
View	Processed	Resume	USAJOBS		01/16/2014 02:31 PM	
	Not Received	Cover Letter				
	Not Received	DD-214				
	Not Received	Other				
	Not Received	Other Veterans Document				

Messages

	Message Type	Date Emailed	Date Printed
View	Notice of Results (NORs)	1/18/2014 1:27:48 AM	
View	Notification Letter	1/21/2014 4:12:24 PM	
View	Acknowledgement Letter	1/16/2014 2:36:29 PM	

Application Processing Status

	Status	Date Submitted

STEP 9

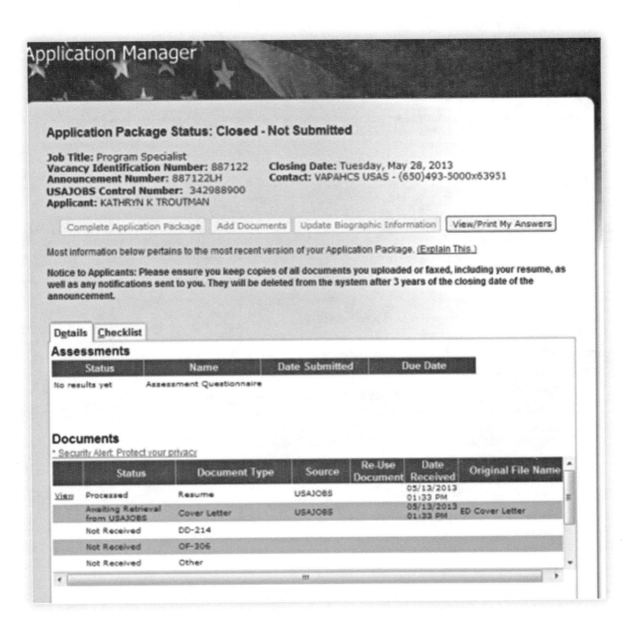

Application Manager

Application Package Status: Closed - Not Submitted

Job Title: Program Specialist
Vacancy Identification Number: 887122
Announcement Number: 887122LH
USAJOBS Control Number: 342988900
Applicant: KATHRYN K TROUTMAN

Closing Date: Tuesday, May 28, 2013
Contact: VAPAHCS USAS - (650)493-5000x63951

[Complete Application Package] [Add Documents] [Update Biographic Information] [View/Print My Answers]

Most information below pertains to the most recent version of your Application Package. (Explain This.)

Notice to Applicants: Please ensure you keep copies of all documents you uploaded or faxed, including your resume, as well as any notifications sent to you. They will be deleted from the system after 3 years of the closing date of the announcement.

Details | **Checklist**

Assessments

Status	Name	Date Submitted	Due Date
No results yet	Assessment Questionnaire		

Documents

* Security Alert: Protect your privacy

	Status	Document Type	Source	Re-Use Document	Date Received	Original File Name
View	Processed	Resume	USAJOBS		05/13/2013 01:33 PM	
	Awaiting Retrieval from USAJOBS	Cover Letter	USAJOBS		05/13/2013 01:33 PM	ED Cover Letter
	Not Received	DD-214				
	Not Received	OF-306				
	Not Received	Other				

Notice of Results (NOR) gives you information about the status of your application. The types of responses could be: Not Eligible, Eligible, Best Qualified, Best Qualified and Not Among the Most Qualified to be Referred, Best Qualified and Referred. It's important to check your NORs, so that you can gauge the success of your applications.

You can find your Notice of Results in Applicationmanager.gov under My Application Packages. Click on the link to open up the announcement and results page. There you will find your messages, including your NORs.

Messages

	Message Type	Date Emailed	Date Printed
View	Cancellation Letter		7/26/2011 12:49:10 PM
View	Notification Letter		6/2/2011 2:25:40 PM

Here are some examples of the types of results you will see when you check your NORs.

Dear KATHRYN K TROUTMAN,

This refers to the application you recently submitted to this office for the position below:

Vacancy ID:	446111
Position:	Human Resources Specialist (Employee Benefits), GS-201-12
Announcement:	11D-123-YS
Agency:	OHCM HumanCapitalManagementDC

Spec Code: 003

Spec Title: US Citizens

Grade: 12

Rating: IE

Referral Name: AP-11-YRS-02020S0

Status: IN - Ineligible

Vet Pref:

Locations:

Washington DC Metro Area, DC

Status Code	Status Message
IN - Ineligible	We have carefully reviewed your application and determined that you are not eligible for the position with this Status code. Please refer to the rating codes and message description.

Rating Code	Rating Message
IE	Your application does not show that you have the length of specialized/specific experience needed for this specialty and grade.

STEP 9

Spec Code:	Spec Title:	Grade:	Rating:
002	Noncompetitive Merit Promotion	15	IAOC

Rating Code:	Rating Message:
IAOC	You are outside the area of consideration.

NOTICE OF RESULTS

Announcement Number 1203039KSDE
Occupation Construction Control Representative
Series/Grade GS-0809G-07
Location Norfolk, VA
Rating 98.61
Veterans Preference NOT A VET
Eligible/Ineligible Not Evaluated

This notice is a record of your application for Federal employment for the vacancy shown above. Under the Office of Personnel Management's regulations for considering applications under Delegated Examining, eligible applicants are considered based on the rating they receive and veteran's preference entitlements.

Your rating (score) shown above is based solely on your answers to the vacancy questions. Because your rating was not within the range for referral for this vacancy, your application was not evaluated for qualifications and your name was not referred to the selecting official for further consideration.

Spec Code:	Spec Title:	Grade:	Rating:
002	Human Resources	04	96
002	Human Resources	05	96
002	Human Resources	06	96
002	Human Resources	07	ID

Rating Code: Rating Message:

ID   You do not meet the minimum education and/or experience requirements for this specialty and grade.

For this vacancy, we referred the names of preference eligible veterans in the top category. Therefore, your name will not be referred to the selecting official at this time. If we receive a request from the program for additional candidates, your application may be reviewed for possible referral.

STEP 10

Interview for a Federal Job

Your first goal for the interview is to stand out above the competition with your relevant skills, experiences, and your ability to communicate them to the hiring manager. Second, you want to impress the hiring team that YOU CAN DO THE JOB being offered. And third, you need to demonstrate confidence, interest, and enthusiasm. This combination of solid relevant content and examples, efficient communications skills, and confident delivery method does not come naturally to most people.

It takes practice, research, and preparation for a successful job interview.

You will see typical questions that could be asked in an interview. Most panel members or individual supervisor/interviewers will prepare seven to ten questions. The same questions are asked of all the interviewees. The answers are graded. So, be prepared to give examples that demonstrate your knowledge, skills, and abilities.

If you have written your KSAs from Step 7, the KSA narrative/examples could be the basis of your accomplishments for the Behavior-Based Interview. But you will have to practice speaking about your accomplishments. Even the most seasoned speakers, briefers, and media experts take training in speaking, presentation, and content development. Jobseekers should spend more time writing examples (their "message") that support their best strengths, and practice speaking these elements. A great interview can get you hired. But interviewing is not easy for anyone.

Be prepared for a new interview format, the Behavior-Based Interview. Be prepared to give examples in answers to seven to ten questions that will be situation or experience based. If you have an example of how you led a team, provided training, or managed a project, be prepared to talk about the project and teamwork. The best answers will be examples that demonstrate your past performance.

Know the paperwork

Know the vacancy announcement, agency mission, and office function. Read your resume and KSAs out loud with enthusiasm. Become convinced that you are very well qualified for the job and that the agency NEEDS you to help achieve their mission.

Do the necessary research

Go online to research the agency, department, and position. Read press releases about the organization. Go to www.washingtonpost.com and search for the organization to see if there are any recent news events.

Practice

In front of a mirror, tape recorder, video camera, family member, friend, anyone who volunteers to listen to you.

Confidence, Knowledge, and Skills

In order to "sell" yourself for a new position, you have to believe in your abilities. Read books and listen to tapes that will help boost your confidence and give you the support you need to "brag" on your work skills. Don't forget or be afraid to use "I"!

Telephone Interview

Prepare as though you are meeting the person in an office. Get dressed nicely, have your papers neatly organized, create a quiet environment, and project a focused listening and communications style. If you are great on the phone, you can get a second interview.

Individual Interview

For the one-on-one interview, get ready for an unknown Q&A format. Prepare your questions and answers ahead of time and be ready. Be friendly, professional, and answer the questions. Practice for this interview.

Group/Panel Interview

Two to six professional staff will interview and observe your answers. This is a difficult interview format, but it is not used too often. Just look at the person asking the question while he or she is speaking. Answer the question by looking at the person asking, but look around the room as well.

Tell Me About Yourself

Write a three-minute introduction that you could use in an interview. It should include information relevant to the position.

A Significant Accomplishment

Write one significant accomplishment that you will describe in an interview:

Select Your Best Competencies

Make a list of your best core competencies:

Write Your Most Critical Skills

Make a list of your best skills that will be most marketable to this employer:

Typical interview questions will be:

J   Job Related
O   Open Ended
B   Behavior-Based
S   Skill and Competency Based

Competency-Based Sample Interview Questions

Often, an interviewer will ask questions that directly relate to a competency required for the position. Here are some examples.

- **Attention to Detail:** Describe a project you were working on that required attention to detail.

- **Communication:** Describe a time when you had to communicate under difficult circumstances.

- **Conflict Management:** Describe a situation where you found yourself working with someone who didn't like you. How did you handle it?

- **Continuous Learning:** Describe a time when you recognized a problem as an opportunity.

- **Customer Service:** Describe a situation in which you demonstrated an effective customer service skill.

- **Decisiveness:** Tell me about a time when you had to stand up for a decision you made even though it made you unpopular.

- **Leadership:** Describe a time when you exhibited participatory management.

- **Planning, Organizing, Goal Setting:** Describe a time when you had to complete multiple tasks. What method did you use to manage your time?

- **Presentation:** Tell me about a time when you developed a lesson, training, or briefing and presented it to a group.

- **Problem Solving:** Describe a time when you analyzed data to determine multiple solutions to a problem. What steps did you take?

- **Resource Management:** Describe a situation when you capitalized on an employee's skill.

- **Team Work:** Describe a time when you had to deal with a team member that was not pulling his/her weight.

Present your best competencies with a great story or example that demonstrates your real behavior.

LEADERSHIP – Inspires, motivates, and guides others toward strategic/operation goals and corporate values. Coaches, mentors, and challenges staff and adapts leadership style to various situations. Consistently demonstrates decisiveness in day-to-day actions. Takes unpopular positions when necessary. Faces adversity head on. Rallies support and strives for consensus to accomplish tasks. Leads by personal example. Demonstrates concern for employees' welfare and safety, by continuously monitoring and eliminating potentially hazardous or unhealthy work situations.

Can you give me an example where you led a team?

CONTEXT:

CHALLENGE:

ACTION:

      1.

      2.

      3.

RESULTS:

Kathryn K. Troutman,
Author and President
The Resume Place, Inc.

Photo by Emily Troutman

1. Founder, President, and Manager of The Resume Place®, the first federal job search consulting and federal resume writing service in the world, and the producer of www.resume-place.com, the first website devoted to federal resume writing.

2. Pioneer designer of the federal resume format in 1995 with the publication of the leading resource for federal human resources and jobseekers worldwide—the *Federal Resume Guidebook*.

3. Developer of the Ten Steps to a Federal Job®, a licensed curriculum and turnkey training program taught by more than 1,000 Certified Federal Job Search Trainers™ (CFJST) around the world.

4. Leading Federal Resume Writing, KSA, Resumix, ECQ and Federal Interview government contracted trainer. GSA Schedule Holder.

5. Author of numerous federal career publications (in addition to the *Federal Resume Guidebook* mentioned above):

The *Military to Federal Career Guide* is the first book for military personnel and is now in its 2nd edition, featuring veteran federal resumes. Troutman recognized the need for returning military personnel from Iraq, Afghanistan, and Kosovo to have a resource available to them in their searches for government jobs.

Ten Steps to a Federal Job was published two months after 9/11 and was written for private industry jobseekers seeking first-time positions in the federal government, where they could contribute to our nation's security. Now in its third edition.

The *Jobseeker's Guide* started initially as the companion course handout to the *Ten Steps* book, but captured its own following when it became the handout text used by over 200 military installations throughout the world for transitioning military and family members. Now in its sixth edition.

With the looming human capital crisis and baby boomers retiring in government, the *Student's Federal Career Guide* was co-authored with Kathryn's daughter and MPP graduate, Emily Troutman, and is the first book for students pursuing a federal job. Now in its third edition, including the latest information on the changing structure of student programs, plus additional guidance for veterans taking advantage of the Post-9/11 GI Bill.

Resumes for Dummies by Joyce Lain Kennedy is renowned as the premier guidebook for resume writing. Kathryn and The Resume Place staff served as designers and producers of all the private industry resume samples for the fifth edition.

Paulina Chen
Designer & Developmental Editor

Paulina was working at the U.S. Environmental Protection Agency when Kathryn came to the EPA to provide federal resume consultations. Kathryn noticed Paulina's ability to communicate complex information in a straightforward, easy-to-understand way. Kathryn offered Paulina her first freelance opportunity—to design and lay out the interior pages for the first edition of *Ten Steps to a Federal Job*. Now many years later, this team is still collaborating, and the *Jobseeker's Guide 6th Edition* is their thirteenth book project together. Paulina also assists The Resume Place and the Federal Career Training Institute with their websites and marketing efforts and is a Certified Federal Job Search Trainer.

Ellen Lazarus
Retired Senior Federal Manager, Human Resources Technical Consultant

Ellen retired as a senior level manager with the U.S. Government where she served as an Assistant Director of the Congressional Research Service, overseeing the operations of the American Law Division and the work of over 50 attorneys. She was also a Senior Specialist in American Public Law. Ellen has assisted numerous veterans with their transition from military to civilian positions. Her expertise includes providing career counseling to military officers and veterans interested in program management, information technology, acquisitions, logistics, and Senior Executive Service managerial positions.

Dennis Eley, Jr.

Wounded Warrior Coordinator, OCHR-San Diego Ops Center

Mr. Dennis Eley, Jr. is a 26 year Navy Veteran from the U.S. Navy. He retired in 2006 at the rank of Chief Warrant Officer (W3). His career with Office of Civilian Human Resources San Diego Operations Center (OCHR SAN) started in January 2010 as a HR Specialist assigned to staffing. Two months later, he was asked to be the full-time Wounded Warrior Coordinator, a new position within the organization and the region. In this role which he still performs today, he provides federal employment support to Wounded Warriors, veterans, and spouses at career fairs, federal resume writing and federal employment process workshops, and during one-on-one interviews.

He also participates in various forums around the nation as a strong advocate for our Wounded Warriors. Dennis and his WW team were recognized for their stellar support of the Wounded Warrior program in the southwest region by the Dept of the Navy, Civilian Human Resources which awarded them the "Community Award for Excellence 2011."

Dennis' background outside of the military and the HRSC includes time with the Employment Development Department (EDD) in various capacities, including as a Career Advisor and Workshop Facilitator. As a facilitator, he developed and implemented a team building workshop titled, "Workplace Success," based on *The Five Dysfunctions of a Team* by Patrick Lencioni.

He holds a B.S. in Human Development from Christian Heritage College, an MBA focus in Leadership from Walden University, and is currently a doctoral student at University of Phoenix.

VETERAN FEDERAL CAREER CONSULTING AND RESUME WRITING SERVICES

We have trained writers who specialize in translating military experience into skills and qualifications for federal positions. We can help you with an outstanding federal resume that can get you referred to a supervisor.

We are pleased to offer America's veterans the following:

- We regularly offer a special 5% discount on veteran career consultation, full service federal resumes, and cover letters.

The Resume Place Resume writers and editors will:

- Review resumes drafted by the veteran
- Determine or confirm best occupational series and grade for the veteran
- Ensure that One Year Specialized Experience is evident for the target positions
- Edit and feature improved keywords for an announcement or classification standard
- Review or confirm accomplishments
- Review and improve format and content
- Finalize the resume in Outline Format with keywords and accomplishments

Get help applying for federal jobs with USAJOBS 3.0:

- USAJOBS 3.0 account and builder setup.
- Document uploads, including veterans' documents, transcripts, cover letter, evaluations.
- Questionnaire review and completion.
- Submission and tracking & follow-up lessons.
- Announcement review for next announcements and job search strategies.

Check out these useful websites:

- *Free Federal Resume Builder, KSA Builder, Cover Letter Builder and Application Writing Builders*
  www.resume-place.com/resources/free-builders/

- *VetFedJobs*
  http://vetfedjobs.org/

- *Feds Hire Vets*
  www.fedshirevets.gov/

- *Mil2FedJobs (State of Maryland)*
  www.dllr.state.md.us/mil2fedjobs/

The
Resume Place

The Resume Place, Inc.
www.resume-place.com
888-480-8265
Federal Resume Writing since 1996
Authors of the first book on Federal Resume Writing:
the *Federal Resume Guidebook*

 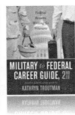    

Order online at www.resume-place.com | Career Center Orders: (410) 744 4324 or (888) 480 8265
FREE SHIPPING to centers and bases in the domestic US and APO; shipping is calculated for HI and overseas

Jobseeker's Guide, 5th Edition

Military to Federal Career Transition Resource
Workbook and guide for the Ten Steps to a Federal
Job® training curriculum. Federal job search strategies
for first-time jobseekers who are separating military
and family members. *$14.95 ea., Bulk Rates Available*

Ten Steps to a Federal Job & CD-ROM, 3rd Ed.

Written for a first-time applicant, particularly those
making a career change from private industry to federal
government. Case studies include 24 before & after
samples of successful resumes! *$14.95 ea., Bulk Rates
Available*

Federal Resume Guidebook & CD-ROM, 5th Ed.

The ultimate guide in federal resume, KSA, and ECQ
writing. 30+ samples on the CD-ROM. Easy to use as
a template for writing. Specialty occupational series
chapters. *$31.95 ea., Bulk Rates Available*

Military to Federal Career Guide & CD-ROM, 2nd Ed.

Federal Resume Writing for Veterans
All samples and insight for military to federal
transition for veterans. Samples are in the Outline
Format with keywords, accomplishments from military
careers. CD-ROM includes all samples and KSAs for
military transition. *$14.95 ea., Bulk Rates Available*

Student's Federal Career Guide, 2nd Ed.

Winner, Best Careers Book of the Year, 2004.
Outstanding book for jobseekers who are just getting
out of college and whose education will help the
applicant get qualified for a position. 20 samples of
recent graduate resumes with emphasis on college
degrees, courses, major papers, internships, and
relevant work experiences. Outstanding usability
of samples on the CD-ROM. *$14.95 ea., Bulk Rates
Available*

Creating Your High School Resume & CD-ROM, 3rd Ed., and Instructor's Guide

Used in high school, military teen career programs,
school-to-work programs worldwide. Samples of
high school resumes—including those targeting
ROTC, College, Certification Programs, Jobs, Military
Scholarship/ Schools. Instructor's CD and Guide with
PPTs and exercises. *$16.95 ea.*

Online Federal Resume Database

This Online Federal Resume Database contains more
than 110 resume samples and federal job search
resources from the current Resume Place publications.
Each CD-ROM has a clearly organized interface.
Sample resumes are available in Word and PDF format
for quick previewing and easy editing. *Individual and
Agency / Base Licenses Available*

★ CERTIFIED FEDERAL JOB SEARCH TRAINER® (CFJST) AND CERTIFIED FEDERAL CAREER COACH® (CFCC) PROGRAM

A few of our 2012 classes

Since 1992, over 1000 other career professionals have benefitted from our unique certification in the Ten Steps to a Federal Job® curriculum, and the program continues to grow each year. Get certified and licensed to teach Kathryn Troutman's popular, proven, turnkey curriculum: Ten Steps to a Federal Job® and Federal Resume & KSA Writing curriculum. This course was developed by Kathryn Troutman as a direct result of her training experiences for hundreds of federal agencies throughout the world.

Our three day program is pre-approved to fulfill 24 continuing education hours for the Center of Credentialing and Education's Global Career Development Facilitator (GCDF) certification.

Registration Benefits - Incredible Value!

- Free Multi-User License to Our Ten Steps Online Resources (three months)
- Online Federal Resume Database
- Ten Steps eLearning Program
- Federal Career Books for Your Library:
  ◊ Federal Resume Guidebook, 5th Edition
  ◊ The New SES Application
  ◊ Jobseeker's Guide, 6th Edition
  ◊ Ten Steps to a Federal Job & CD-ROM, 3rd Edition
  ◊ Military to Federal Career Guide & CD-ROM, 2nd Edition
  ◊ The Student's Federal Career Guide, 3rd Edition
  ◊ Creating Your High School Resume & CD-ROM
  ◊ Beautiful Ten Steps bag
- PowerPoint Presentations:
  ◊ Ten Steps to a Federal Job® – Licensed for two years
  ◊ Federal Hiring Program
  ◊ Veteran's and Spouse Hiring Programs
  ◊ Student Federal Hiring Programs

"I just wanted to let you know that attendance at the 3 - day course in March [2012] has done wonders for my confidence and wonders for my clients. When we go through the OPM Job Factors and the Grading of GS positions, most clients are over-joyed to have opened the "treasure chest" where the mystery of pursuing a Federal Job Position is solved. Thank you for all that you do!! I love the books and find something new EVERY day that I can share with my fellow coaches."

More Information and Registration

www.fedjobtraining.com/certification-programs.htm